SBAC
SMARTER BALANCED
GRADE 8 ELA

By Kim Lohse

BARRON'S

About the Author

Kim Lohse has been teaching English and creative writing for more than 20 years, and the last twelve of those years have been in Palo Alto, California. She received a B.A. in English from Hunter College and an M.F.A. in poetry from Vermont College. In addition to teaching, Kim Lohse writes poetry and translates French surrealist essays and poetry. She lives in Redwood City, California with her wonderful partner, Paul, her two children, Sarah and Erik, and far too many cats, dogs, and chickens.

Acknowledgments

Thank you to all my former students who have helped me hone my teaching methods, and thank you to all my many teaching mentors and colleagues. Thank you also to my family, in particular, Maureen and John Schaffner, who helped me create time for this project. I have extra special gratitude for Deborah Adams, my long-time classroom aide, light, muse, and fine editor.

—Kim Lohse

The Smarter Balanced screenshots, on pages 3, 4, and 6, as well as the Smarter Balanced Performance Task Scoring Rubrics on pages 203–215, are reprinted with permission courtesy of The Regents of the University of California. The publishing of this information does not represent an endorsement of products offered or solicited by Barron's Educational Series, Inc.

All inquiries should be addressed to:
Barron's Educational Series, Inc.
250 Wireless Boulevard
Hauppauge, NY 11788
www.barronseduc.com

ISBN: 978-1-4380-1062-5
Library of Congress Control Number: 2017953370

Date of Manufacture: December 2017
Manufactured by: B11R11

Printed in the United States of America
9 8 7 6 5 4 3 2 1

10%
POST-CONSUMER WASTE
Paper contains a minimum of 10% post-consumer waste (PCW). Paper used in this book was derived from certified, sustainable forestlands.

Contents

Introduction

SBAC Overview

In the spring of your eighth-grade year, you will have to take a formative test referred to as the SBAC, which stands for the Smarter Balanced Assessment Consortium. This test measures the full range of your abilities in the Common Core Standards learned during eighth grade. While you will be tested in other subjects, this test preparation guide concentrates on the SBAC Grade 8 English Language Arts (ELA) exam. On this exam, you will be tested on reading, writing, listening, speaking, and conducting research. You will receive an overall ELA scaled score (range) as well as four other scores that are broken down by claims.

The SBAC Grade 8 ELA Exam

The SBAC Grade 8 ELA exam is broken into three sessions. You will take the **English Language Arts Computer Adaptive Test** (ELA CAT) in one session that lasts approximately an hour and a half. The **English Language Arts Performance Task** (ELA PT) is broken into two sessions. The first session, called the Performance Task Lesson, is short—usually about 30 minutes. This is an instructive session with a teacher that is meant to orient students to the Performance Task. The second session is the actual Performance Task, which lasts around two hours. Please note that this test is usually scheduled around the same time as the SBAC Grade 8 Math exam, as seen in Table I-1.

The SBAC has a recommended time allotted for each session, but *remember that these are not timed tests*. Although the sample schedule in Table I-1 shows that there is 1 hour and 30 minutes for the ELA Computer Adaptive Test on Monday, you may take more or less time since that time allotment is only an approximate. You should feel free to take as much time as you need to complete each part of these tests. Be aware that, if you need more time, the test administrator may move you to a different location to complete the test. There are some rules for taking breaks, which will be discussed later in the Universal Tools section of this introduction.

Keep in mind that, during the same testing session, each student will be taking a very different test since the computer adapts the test to the individual. Do not be discouraged if other students are finishing before you or if you are finishing ahead of others since your test is likely to be very different from that of the person sitting next to you.

Table I-1. Sample SBAC Grade 8 Testing Schedule

Monday	Tuesday	Wednesday	Thursday	Friday
ELA: Computer Adaptive Test (1 hour, 30 minutes)	Math: Computer Adaptive Test (2 hours)	ELA: Performance Task Lesson (30 minutes)	ELA: Performance Task (2 hours) Math: Performance Task Lesson (30 minutes)	Math: Performance Task (1 hour, 30 minutes)

Task Types

The SBAC uses four types of tasks: **selected-response tasks**, **technology-enhanced tasks**, **constructed-response tasks**, and a **Performance Task**. This guide contains four review chapters that will help you become acquainted with each of these task types. These can't all be called "questions" because the SBAC often asks you to execute a task, such as clicking on a misspelled word or reordering sentences, and only occasionally asks you to answer questions.

Selected-response tasks, technology-enhanced tasks, and constructed-response tasks are *computer adaptive*. This means that if you answer a CAT task correctly, the next task will be adjusted to the next level, or it could stay on the same level as the previous task. If you answer a CAT item incorrectly, the level could stay the same or drop. The test continues to adapt to the right level for you; it is for this reason that you cannot skip ahead on this test. The computer adaptive nature of the exam allows the SBAC to test you more quickly and more completely. The difficulty of the task determines the weight given to the task in terms of scoring and is taken into account in the scaling of your result. A high-scaled task performed correctly will contribute to a higher overall scaled score, whereas a low-scaled task will not help your score as much. While this might seem complicated, the most important part to remember is to take your time and try your best. Note that the Performance Task is not computer adaptive.

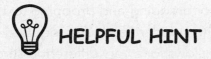

HELPFUL HINT

Computer Adaptive means that the questions you encounter on the CAT part of the test are determined by how you answer each question. Remember, the CAT is designed to adapt to *you*.

During the ELA CAT, the selected-response tasks, the technology-enhanced tasks, and the constructed-response tasks can be introduced in any order. For example, you could encounter a constructed-response task followed by a selected-response task followed by a technology-enhanced task. For most of the test, you will see a text on the left side of the screen and the task on the right side of the screen. Let's take a closer look at each of the four task types:

1. Selected-Response Tasks

Selected-response tasks are classic multiple-choice questions. Typically, each correct answer is given one point. Chapter 1 discusses how these tasks are constructed and provides strategies for answering them along with sample tasks.

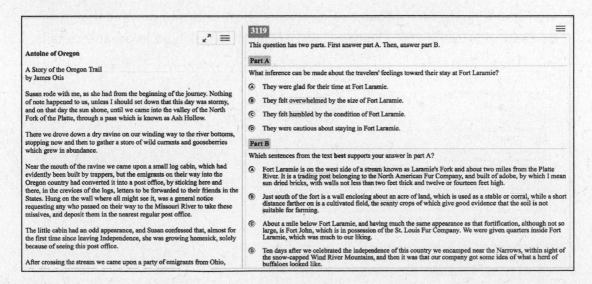

Figure I-1. Example of a selected-response task

2. Technology-Enhanced Tasks

Sometimes referred to as *nontraditional response questions*, technology-enhanced tasks require computer technology to answer the questions. Examples include clicking on a sentence, editing text, or dragging-and-dropping text from one location to another. The old way of taking standardized tests required only a pencil and paper; this new way of testing allows for a very different testing experience. If you use computers regularly, you will not find the technology very complicated. Chapter 2 goes into greater detail about these technology-enhanced tasks. Typically, each correct answer is given one point.

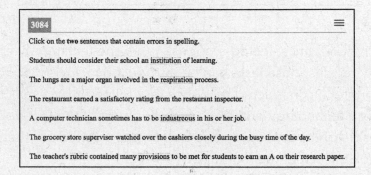

Figure I-2. Example of a technology-enhanced task

3. Constructed-Response Tasks

Constructed-response tasks require you to demonstrate your writing skills. Often, the task will ask you to read a passage and write a paragraph in response. Sometimes this is analytical; other times it is creative. Typically, you are provided with a stimulus: a text, a source (e.g., a video clip), and/or a graphic that corresponds to the task. Chapter 3 will explain this task type in greater detail.

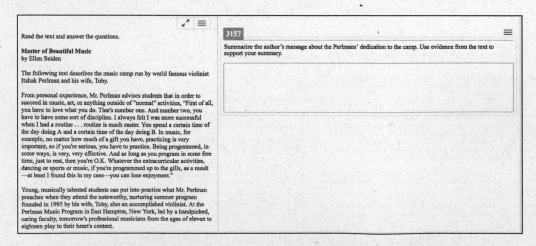

Figure I-3. Example of a constructed-response task

The scoring for these tasks uses a tiered point system based on specific criteria for that particular task. For instance, the item may ask you to write a short-answer response in which you state your opinion, and your response would be scored on a rubric like the one in Table I-2.

Table I-2. Sample Scoring Rubric for a Constructed-Response Task

2 Points	This response: > provides an adequate conclusion that follows from and supports the preceding information in the body or provides a description as to why this information is important or what should happen next > does more than restate the points/reasons—it is not formulaic > provides adequate connections and/or a progression of ideas that contributes to coherence
1 Point	This response: > provides a limited conclusion that is related to the information in the body of writing > lists, restates, or summarizes the points/reasons—it is formulaic
0 Points	This response: > provides no conclusion or a conclusion that is minimally related to the information in the body of writing > may restate random and/or incorrect details from the preceding information > does not provide connections or a progression of ideas

4. Performance Task

The Performance Task part of the test allows you to go into more depth in a variety of ways to demonstrate your critical-thinking skills. Chapter 4 will provide a clear overview of the Performance Task. The Performance Task begins with an introductory lesson between the teacher and the class to familiarize everyone with the task at hand. During the actual Performance Task, you will answer a number of questions and complete activities that are all connected to a single theme or scenario. These activities will measure your writing and research skills and your depth of understanding. Think of this part of the SBAC as the long writing section since you will likely be asked to write an essay or a narrative. You will also need to complete a handful of smaller tasks or questions.

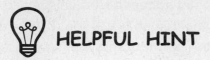

HELPFUL HINT

Remember, the Performance Task is *not* computer adaptive.

This portion of the test is very different from the ELA CAT. Each Performance Task will have its own rubric scoring system based on the content. There will likely be several constructed-response tasks in addition to a large writing task (typically an essay or a story). The constructed-response tasks use a tiered point system. The larger writing task is scored using a rubric based on a 0-4 score range. The Smarter Balanced Performance Task Scoring Rubrics can be found in Appendix A of this book.

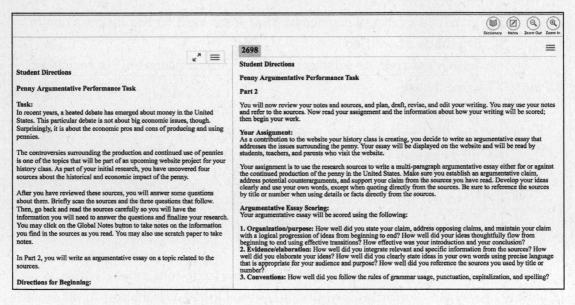

Figure I-4. Example of a Performance Task

Scoring

Scaled Scores

A scaled score is your overall numerical score. These scores fall on a continuous scale (from approximately 2000 to 3000) that increases across grade levels. Scaled scores can be used to illustrate your current level of achievement and growth over time. For more information about scaled scores, visit

www.smarterbalanced.org/assessments/scores/

Achievement Levels

Based on your scaled score, you will fall into one of four categories of performance called **achievement levels**.

Achievement Level Descriptors

Achievement levels are defined by achievement level descriptors, the specifications for what knowledge and skills students display at each level (i.e., Level 1, Level 2, Level 3, and Level 4). Table I-3 below shows the range of scaled scores for each achievement level.

Table I-3. Achievement Levels

Level 4	The student *has exceeded* the achievement standard and demonstrates advanced progress toward mastery of the knowledge and skills in English Language Arts/literacy needed for likely success in entry-level, credit-bearing college coursework after high school.
Level 3	The student *has met* the achievement standard and demonstrates progress toward mastery of the knowledge and skills in English Language Arts/literacy needed for likely success in entry-level, credit-bearing college coursework after high school.
Level 2	The student *has nearly met* the achievement standard and may require further development to demonstrate the knowledge and skills in English Language Arts/literacy needed for likely success in entry-level, credit-bearing college coursework after high school.
Level 1	The student *has not met* the achievement standard and needs substantial improvement to demonstrate the knowledge and skills in English Language Arts/literacy needed for likely success in entry-level, credit-bearing college coursework after high school.

The SBAC refers to these categories as levels, but each Smarter Balanced member state refers to them in different ways, such as "novice, developing, proficient, and advanced." Students performing at Levels 3 and 4 are considered on track to demonstrating the knowledge and skills necessary for college and career readiness. Additionally, you will receive a score of 1–3 for each of the four major claim areas. However, you will not learn the exact score for any question or task. For more information about achievement level descriptors, visit

www.smarterbalanced.org/assessments/scores/

SBAC Claims

The SBAC claims are the overall goals and purpose of the test. Every task and question on the test measures your ability to demonstrate at least one of the four skills listed in Table I-4.

Table I-4. SBAC Claims

Claim 1	Students can read closely and analytically to comprehend a range of increasingly complex literary and informational texts.
Claim 2	Students can produce effective and well-grounded writing for a range of purposes and audiences.
Claim 3	Students can employ effective speaking and listening skills for a range of purposes and audiences.
Claim 4	Students can engage in research/inquiry to investigate topics and to analyze, integrate, and present information.

A sample student report would read:

Scaled Score: 2701	
Level 4: Exceeded Standard	
Claim 1—Reading	Above standard
Claim 2—Writing	Above standard
Claim 3—Listening	Above standard
Claim 4—Research/Inquiry	At or near standard

Beginning the Test Session

The SBAC is taken on a computer, and the testing administrator (usually your teacher) also uses a computer. Depending on which test session you are sitting for, the administrator may also give you scratch paper, a pencil, a dictionary, and/or a thesaurus. The administrator will open the test session on your computer. You will need to log in using a unique code given to you by the administrator. The computer will then give you a sound-check prompt. Once you have heard the tones and adjusted the volume, you will begin the test.

Ending the Test Session

Once you have completed all the tasks in the test session, you will be given a prompt asking if you wish to end the session. Once you answer yes, it will prompt you to confirm one more time to be sure. By answering that you wish to end the session on the second prompt, you will end the session, and the administrator will not be able to reopen the test session for you. Note that you can end the test session before you complete all of the test segments, but *those unanswered questions will be scored as incorrect*.

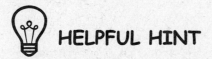 HELPFUL HINT

Since any unanswered questions will count against you, be careful not to end the test session accidentally. If you need to take a break to use the restroom, for example, be sure to follow the break-taking procedures so as not to end the test session accidentally, which will prevent you from resuming the test. Ask the administrator about any break-taking procedures before starting the test.

Technology

All parts of the SBAC are taken on a computer. If you are not used to working on a computer, now's the time to practice! The SBAC assumes that you are able to type quickly enough to complete the test. If your typing is slow, you may want to practice typing to increase your ability. There are a number of typing tutorials available online, many of which are free. Depending on what type of computer you will use at school, you should practice using a mouse or a track pad. All of the tasks on this test require you to navigate, answer questions, and perform tasks using a mouse or a track pad. The tasks could include different types of media, so if you are watching a video or listening to something, for example, you will need to use headphones. You will need to be able to start, stop, and rewind a video on the computer, which you can practice on any number of websites. The test makers assume that you will be very comfortable using this technology to take this test.

Universal Tools

Using a computer to take a test has some advantages. The SBAC has universal tools to help you while you are taking the test. There are two categories of tools you should familiarize yourself with: **embedded** and **non-embedded universal tools**. The embedded tools are part of the computer program, while the non-embedded tools are outside of the computer program. Knowing how to use both of these kinds of tools will help you take the test, especially during the more complicated parts. For instance, you may want to copy part of a reading passage and paste it onto the notepad because you would like to quote from that section of the passage later, or you may want to highlight key words or ideas in a reading passage. Most of the tools feature easy to follow icons. Be aware that some of these tools may slow you down, so use them wisely.

Embedded Tools

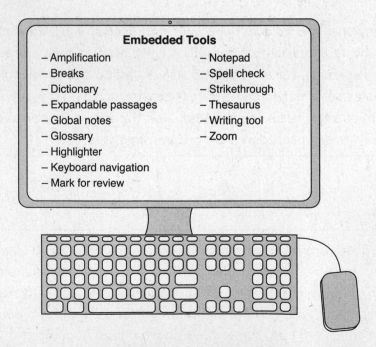

Embedded Tools

– Amplification
– Breaks
– Dictionary
– Expandable passages
– Global notes
– Glossary
– Highlighter
– Keyboard navigation
– Mark for review

– Notepad
– Spell check
– Strikethrough
– Thesaurus
– Writing tool
– Zoom

Figure I-5. Embedded tools

The following tools will be available within the computer testing program.

Tool	How It Works
amplification	You will be able to adjust the volume using the computer or the headphones.
breaks	You will be able to take a break. You will have to pause the computer to do this and then the test administrator will need to reopen the session. **If you take a break longer than 50 minutes, the session will close. The test administrator will need to reopen the session, but you will not be able to return to any sections that you worked on previously.**
dictionary	During the Performance Task only, you will be able to use an online English dictionary. You can use this dictionary to help with spelling or to look up the definition of a word.
expandable passages	The text and the questions will be presented side by side on the screen, and you will be able to expand one side or the other, which may help you focus on one part more easily.
global notes	During the Performance Task, a digital notepad will be available for you to use. This is like online scratch paper. As you move through the various sections of the Performance Task, you will be able to access the notes you have taken. As you finish a section, you will not be able to go back to reread questions or change your answers, but you will be able to see and use the notes you have taken. This feature is unique to the Performance Task only. This is a tremendous tool to use when you are planning and writing your essay or narrative. Note that the global notes are different from the notepad, which is available on the CAT portion of this test.
glossary	For some key words, indicated with a gray line either above or below the word in a passage, a definition will be provided for you via an English glossary. By clicking on or hovering over the word, a pop-up window will appear with the word's definition.

Tool	How It Works
highlighter	A digital highlighter will be available for marking any text, questions, or answer choices. **Once you move on to the next segment of the test, or if you take a break for longer than 50 minutes, the highlighting will not be saved.** Note that physical highlighters will not be permitted in the testing session and cannot be used on the scratch paper. Only pencils may be used on the scratch paper.
keyboard navigation	In addition to using a mouse to move through the test, you will also be able to use the keyboard to navigate the test (via the arrow keys).
mark for review	You will be able to flag questions for review, which allows you to move through a segment of the test and then come back to a question that you would like to review once more. **Markings will not be saved once you move to the next segment of the test or after you have paused the test for more than 50 minutes.**
notepad	During the CAT, a digital notepad will be available for you to use. This is like online scratch paper for you to type notes on. **When you move on to the next segment of the test or when you take a break for longer than 50 minutes, the notes will not stay saved.** Note that while the notepad is similar to the global notes, the global notes are only available during the Performance Task, and the notepad is only available during each section of the CAT. Keep in mind that when you move on to each new section of the CAT, the notepad will clear, and the notes that you took during the previous section of the CAT will no longer be available for you to review.
spell check	This tool for checking the spelling of words will only be available during the Performance Task. Spell check only gives an indication that a word is misspelled; it does not provide the correct spelling.
strikethrough	Using the strikethrough tool, you will be able to cross out answer choices to help you narrow down the options for the correct answer. If an answer choice is an image, a strikethrough line will not appear, but the image will be grayed out.

Tool	How It Works
thesaurus	During the second session of the Performance Task (the writing part), a digital thesaurus will be provided. This thesaurus can help you find synonyms of words or help you introduce more exciting word choices in your writing.
writing tool	This tool is actually several tools combined. You can use this tool to cut and paste, copy, underline, italicize, bold, undo-redo, and insert bullet points into your writing. You will be familiar with all of these tools if you have used a computer word processing program before.
zoom	You will be able to zoom in and zoom out on text and graphics. The default font size for the test is 14 pt.

Non-Embedded Tools

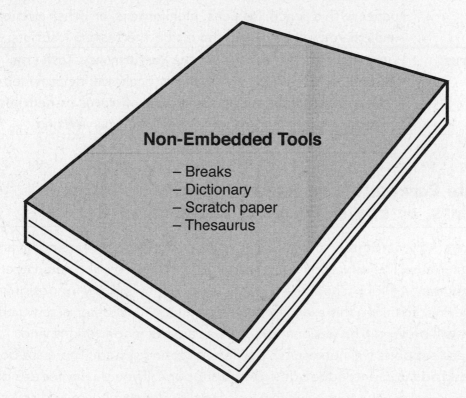

Figure I-6. Non-embedded tools

The following tools will be available to you outside of the computer testing program.

Tool	How It Works
breaks	You will be able to take a break. You will have to pause the computer to do this and then the test administrator will need to reopen the session. **If you take a break longer than 50 minutes, the session will close. The test administrator will need to reopen the session, but you will not be able to return to any sections that you worked on previously.**
dictionary	During the second session of the Performance Task (the writing part), you will be provided with a physical English dictionary (book) to look up the spelling or definition of a word.
scratch paper	You will be given scratch paper and a pencil to write notes on or to plan your responses. Scratch paper and notes may not leave the testing location. You can only write on the scratch paper with a pencil. No pens, highlighters, or other writing implements will be permitted inside the testing location.
thesaurus	During the second session of the Performance Task (the writing part), a physical thesaurus (book) will be provided. This thesaurus can help you find synonyms of words or help you introduce more exciting word choices in your writing.

Note to Parents of Students with IEPs, 504 Plans, or English Language Learners

There are additional supports, called "designated supports," that are not available to most students. The education team, made up of informed educators, parents, and the student, at your school site determines student eligibility for designated supports. Prior to taking this exam, the education team must determine which supports will be used. The designated supports are not modifications, and using these supports will not result in a different scoring system. There are both embedded and non-embedded designated supports. If you qualify for designated supports, you may want to meet with your school's education team to discuss how to practice using these additional supports prior to taking the test. Ideally, you should be very familiar with any determined designated supports as part of your regular instruction.

How to Use This Test Prep Guide

This guide is designed to help you better understand the SBAC Grade 8 ELA exam and to provide you with practice and strategies for achieving success on this test. It will provide you with an overview of this exam and then go into more detail on the different types of tasks you will encounter on test day. Test-taking strategies are provided for each type of task. There are also sample tasks and questions within each review chapter that illustrate the different task types; answers with explanations are provided in Chapter 6. Additionally, Chapter 5 contains a full-length practice test complete with both parts of the exam: a **Computer Adaptive Test** (CAT) and a **Performance Task**. Both parts of this practice test use SBAC-style vocabulary and questions that are designed to mirror those on the actual exam. Answers to all questions on both parts of this practice test can be found in Chapter 6. Appendix A reviews all of the Smarter Balanced Performance Task Scoring Rubrics so that you'll be fully aware of what readers will be looking for in your written responses on the Performance Task. Although this guide is not designed to be a comprehensive review of the Common Core Standards, many of the Common Core Standards were used to construct the sample questions and the practice test. A complete list of the Grade 8 ELA Common Core Standards is located in Appendix B. Finally, a glossary provides you with key terms that you should be familiar with when taking this test.

It will take some time to become familiar with each portion of the test, so allow yourself plenty of time to study. Form a study plan. Break your study sessions into parts. Table I-5 provides a sample study schedule.

Table I-5. Sample Study Schedule

Study Session 1	Introduction Chapter 1 Chapter 2
Study Session 2	Chapter 3
Study Session 3	Chapter 4
Study Session 4	Take the CAT portion of the practice test
Study Session 5	Take the Performance Task portion of the practice test
Study Session 6	Review the answer explanations for both sections of the practice test to determine what you know and what you need to review further

Read each chapter of this book to become familiar with each portion of the test. Use a highlighter and take notes to help you remember what you have learned. Practice the strategies from each chapter. Attempt the sample tasks and consult the answer explanations in Chapter 6 to see what you know and what you need to review further. When taking the practice test, set aside the recommended amount of time, and take the test in an environment as free of distractions as possible since you want to mimic actual testing conditions. Once you've completed this book, be sure to continue studying by reading a variety of texts (especially informative texts) to develop your highlighting, annotating, and note-taking skills.

Helpful Hints

Throughout the chapters in this book, you will see Helpful Hints that will give you important reminders along the way. Pay attention to those hints because you may need them on test day!

Selected-Response Tasks

Overview

Selected-response tasks are essentially multiple-choice questions. Sometimes selected-response tasks will be mixed with technology-enhanced tasks or constructed-response tasks for the same stimulus text. Chapters 2 and 3 will provide more details about these other two task types.

Each selected-response task has three parts, although they are not labeled. The first part is the overview that contains the directions for completing the task and gives context to the reading. The second part is the stimulus text or non-text item. This text can be from any genre. You may encounter a poem, a narrative, or an informative text. You may also be given some other form of media, such as video clips, audio clips, graphs, charts, images, or research topics. You may use many of your universal tools when working with non-text items. The third part is the actual task or questions followed by a series of answer choices. Note that sometimes you may be required to click on more than one answer, so be sure to read the questions very carefully so that you know exactly what the question is asking and so that you can respond correctly. You will be given one point for each correct answer.

Strategies

1. Orientation

Read the overview, the questions, and the tasks carefully first (skipping the stimulus text or non-text item for now). This will give you an idea of where you are heading and what you will be asked to keep an eye out for when reading the stimulus text. Match key words to key ideas, and look for key words that will tell you exactly what the question is looking for. Use the highlighter tool to mark the key words. Page 18 contains a list of common verbs and a list of common nouns that will likely be used for selected-response questions and tasks. Be sure that you are familiar with the meaning of each word.

Verbs

analyze	demonstrate	examine	predict
apply	describe	explain	retell
articulate	determine	identify	revise
cite	develop	infer	suggest
click	discuss	integrate	summarize
compare	distinguish	interpret	support
compose	edit	justify	synthesize
contrast	evaluate	locate	trace

Nouns

adjective	evidence	simile
analogy	figurative language	stanza
argument	illustration	structure
cause (and effect)	interaction	theme
central idea	metaphor	tone
claim	mood	verb
connection	point of view	
details	rhetoric	

2. Read the Stimulus Material

Read the stimulus text thoughtfully. Using your universal tools, you can expand the text to help focus on the reading passage specifically. Pay special attention to any text features. For example, bolded, italicized, or underlined words are likely to be important to the task. You should also use the highlighter and notepad in your universal tools to make notes that identify important parts of the text that will help you with your responses. You might be asked to watch a video or look at a picture instead of reading a text. In that case, pay careful attention to what is said or what is shown because you will likely be asked to recall and analyze these non-text items when you answer the task and questions at hand.

3. Reread the Questions and Narrow Down the Answer Choices

Reread the tasks and questions, and begin to eliminate answer choices. Answer any easy questions first, and note any key words or important ideas. Use your universal strikethrough tool to cross out wrong answer choices. Usually, you can spot one or two silly or obviously incorrect answer choices right away. Refer back to the text as you need to. Hopefully, you can narrow it down to the right answer, but if you are not certain, guess. Guessing between two answer choices still gives you a fifty percent chance of getting the right answer. If you aren't certain of your guess, you can mark the question for review and come back to it. Sometimes other questions will provide hints to help you figure out more information about the difficult question that you were working on.

HELPFUL HINT

If you aren't certain of your guess, you can mark the question for review and come back to it. Sometimes other questions will provide hints to help you figure out more information about the more difficult questions in that section.

Practice Exercises

Now it is time to practice these strategies. While you do not have access to all the universal tools, you can mimic several of them. Highlight and annotate the text. Take notes on a separate sheet of paper, if you need to. Cross out eliminated answer choices. For each task, orient yourself first, and then read the stimulus text carefully. Finally, reread the tasks and questions and eliminate answer choices. The correct answers and explanations can be found in Chapter 6.

HELPFUL HINT

On the actual exam, the passages, and the questions that accompany them, will be placed in a side-by-side scrollable format. This side-by-side format will allow you to easily refer back to the passage for textual evidence.

Exercise 1

College and Career Readiness Anchor Standard for Reading R.1

Read closely to determine what the text says explicitly and to make logical inferences from it; cite specific textual evidence when writing or speaking to support conclusions drawn from the text.

College and Career Readiness Anchor Standard for Reading R.5

Analyze the structure of texts, including how specific sentences, paragraphs, and larger portions of the text (e.g., a section, chapter, scene, or stanza) relate to each other and the whole.

Common Core Standard RI.8.2

Determine a central idea of a text and analyze its development over the course of the text, including its relationship to supporting ideas; provide an objective summary of the text.

Common Core Standard RI.8.5

Analyze in detail the structure of a specific paragraph in a text, including the role of particular sentences in developing and refining a key concept.

Common Core Standard W.8.1.A

Introduce claim(s), acknowledge and distinguish the claim(s) from alternate or opposing claims, and organize the reasons and evidence logically.

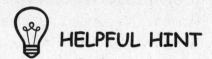 HELPFUL HINT

You must respond to all tasks in a section before you can move on to the next section.

Directions: For his physical education class, Kevin is writing an explanatory essay about how to start running to get healthy. Read the draft of his essay below, and then answer questions 1–3.

Everyone knows that good health requires exercise, and running is a simple and effective way to do this. This can be intimidating for some people because it seems too hard. Running isn't hard at all if you start smart and make a plan. Most doctors recommend that we get at least 30 minutes of cardio exercise in three times a week. Running a 5K race is a good example. The distance is not very far. An average runner can run five kilometers in about 30 to 40 minutes. First, you should think about what sort of habit you want to establish and set a realistic goal. Then, you should think about what your initial endurance is. Can you run a block? Or maybe you can walk a mile? Increase your starting distance or time a little each day until you can run five kilometers. Next, set aside a time each day to do your workout. If you don't have a set time, it will be harder to find the time. Put it on your calendar, and plan around your workout. Staying motivated is also hard. As part of the plan, build in a reinforcement system. For instance, you can buy a new pair of running socks once you can run three kilometers without stopping or have completed two weeks of workouts. If you set a goal and make a plan, establishing a new habit should be easier.

1. Kevin wants to revise the underlined part of his essay to make the steps for the plan clearer. Select the best way to reorder the sentences.

   O A. An average runner can run five kilometers in about 30 to 40 minutes. Running a 5K race is a good example. First, you should think about what sort of habit you want to establish and set a realistic goal. The distance is not very far.

   O B. First, you should think about what sort of habit you want to establish and set a realistic goal. Running a 5K race is a good example. The distance is not very far. An average runner can run five kilometers in about 30 to 40 minutes.

   O C. An average runner can run five kilometers in about 30 to 40 minutes. First, you should think about what sort of habit you want to establish and set a realistic goal. Running a 5K race is a good example. The distance is not very far.

   O D. Running a 5K race is a good example. An average runner can run five kilometers in about 30 to 40 minutes. First, you should think about what sort of habit you want to establish and set a realistic goal. The distance is not very far.

2. Identify which of the following sentences is the main claim of Kevin's essay.

   O A. As part of the plan, build in a reinforcement system.
   O B. Most doctors recommend that we get at least 30 minutes of cardio exercise in three times a week.
   O C. Running isn't hard at all if you start smart and make a plan.
   O D. If you don't have a set time, it will be harder to find the time.

3. Reread the following sentence from the text, and complete the task.

   "As part of the plan, build in a reinforcement system."

   Identify which of the following words would be a strong synonym for the underlined word.

   O A. reward
   O B. strength
   O C. persuasive
   O D. dual

(Answers are on page 149.)

Exercise 2

College and Career Readiness Anchor Standard for Reading R.7

Integrate and evaluate content presented in diverse media and formats, including visually and qualitatively, as well as in words.

Common Core Standard RI.8.7

Evaluate the advantages and disadvantages of using different mediums (e.g., print or digital text, video, multimedia) to present a particular topic or idea.

Common Core Standard W.8.1.B

Support claim(s) with logical reasoning and relevant evidence, using accurate, credible sources and demonstrating an understanding of the topic or text.

Common Core Standard L.8.1

Demonstrate command of the conventions of standard English grammar and usage when writing or speaking.

Directions: Maria is creating a flyer for her dog walking business. Read the draft below, and complete questions 1 and 2.

City Sniffers

Do you have an energetic dog?
Do you need a little more time in your day?

Call Maria!

I love dogs and have a lot of experience. I have been a dog owner my whole life. I have been walking dogs professionally for four years. <u>Let me take your pooch for a tour of the neighborhood soon, you can put your feet up and relax.</u>

References available

---

1. Maria spotted an error on her flyer. Select which of the following choices is *not* a solution to the grammar issue in the underlined sentence.

   O A. Let me take your pooch for a tour of the neighborhood soon, so you can put your feet up and relax.

   O B. Let me take your pooch for a tour of the neighborhood soon; you can put your feet up and relax.

   O C. Let me take your pooch for a tour of the neighborhood soon. You can put your feet up and relax.

   O D. Let me take your pooch for a tour of the neighborhood soon so you can put your feet up and relax.

2. Maria's flyer is missing some information. Select which information would be *best* to include on the flyer.

   O A. Maria's phone number
   O B. the price of Maria's service
   O C. the places in the neighborhood she walks the dogs
   O D. how many dogs Maria has owned

(Answers are on page 150.)

Exercise 3

College and Career Readiness Anchor Standard for Language L.5

Demonstrate understanding of figurative language, word relationships, and nuances in word meanings.

Common Core Standard RL.8.2

Determine a theme or central idea of a text and analyze its development over the course of the text, including its relationship to the characters, setting, and plot; provide an objective summary of the text.

Common Core Standard RL.8.4

Determine the meaning of words and phrases as they are used in a text, including figurative and connotative meanings; analyze the impact of specific word choices on meaning and tone, including analogies or allusions to other texts.

Common Core Standard RL.8.10

By the end of the year, read and comprehend literature, including stories, dramas, and poems, at the high end of grades 6–8 text complexity band independently and proficiently.

Directions: Read the poem "A Good Play," by Robert Louis Stevenson, and complete questions 1 and 2.

A Good Play

by Robert Louis Stevenson

We built a ship upon the stairs,

All made of the back-bedroom chairs,

And filled it full of sofa pillows

To go a-sailing on the billows.

We took a saw and several nails,

And water in the nursery pails;

And Tom said, "Let us also take

An apple and a slice of cake;"—

Which was enough for Tom and me

To go a-sailing on, till tea.

We sailed along for days and days,

And had the very best of plays;

But Tom fell out and hurt his knee,

So there was no one left but me.

1. Select which of the following lines best represents the theme of the poem.

    O A. "We built a ship upon the stairs"

    O B. "And had the very best of plays"

    O C. "So there was no one left but me"

    O D. "All made of the back-bedroom chairs"

2. Select the point of view that this poem is mostly likely told from.

    O A. a parent watching children play

    O B. a nursery nanny observing children play

    O C. a child who is playing

    O D. an adult remembering a time of playing

(Answers are on page 150.)

Technology-Enhanced Tasks

CHAPTER 2

Overview

Technology-enhanced tasks can only be performed on a computer since they require computer technology to be completed. Familiarizing yourself with a computer will be helpful. You must know how to use a mouse and a keyboard effectively to complete these tasks, which will be presented along with selected-response and constructed-response tasks.

Similar to the selected-response tasks, each technology-enhanced task has three parts, although they are not labeled. The first part will provide context for the stimulus text and directions for completing the task at hand. The stimulus text or non-text item is the second part. A text could be from any genre, and a non-text item could be a picture or a video. Most often, however, you will be working with a stimulus text. The third part is the actual task or questions themselves including answer choices where applicable.

For these tasks, you may be asked to click on a sentence or a word within the stimulus text, or you may be asked to select an item from a drop-down menu. The task could also ask you to drag-and-drop notes or sentences into a new order. Some tasks will be simple and straightforward. Others may require multiple steps. Most tasks are worth one point. You will need to complete all tasks in a section before you move to the next section.

 HELPFUL HINT

If you are struggling to get the technology to work, take that as a hint that you may not be answering the question correctly. For instance, if the task asks you to click on a certain type of sentence but the computer will not let you select a specific sentence, you might not be selecting the correct sentence. The SBAC will always allow you to select the right answer available among many incorrect choices.

Strategies

1. Orientation

Read the overview, the questions, and the tasks carefully first (skipping the stimulus text or non-text item for now). This will give you an idea of what sort of task you are being asked to perform. Match key words to key ideas, and look for key words that will tell you exactly what the question is looking for. Use the highlighter tool to mark the key words. Below is a list of common verbs, followed by a list of common nouns on page 31, that will likely be used for technology-enhanced questions and tasks. Be sure that you are familiar with the meaning of each word.

Verbs			
analyze	define	explain	respond
apply	demonstrate	identify	retell
argue	describe	illustrate	revise
articulate	determine	infer	state
cite	develop	integrate	suggest
click	discuss	interpret	summarize
compare	distinguish	justify	support
compose	edit	locate	synthesize
contrast	evaluate	persuade	trace
critique	examine	predict	

Nouns		
adjective	details	point of view
analogy	evidence	rhetoric
argument	figurative language	simile
cause (and effect)	illustration	stanza
central idea	interaction	structure
claim	metaphor	theme
connection	mood	tone

2. Read the Stimulus Material

If you are presented with a text, read the stimulus text carefully. Use your universal tools to expand the text to help focus on the reading passage specifically. Pay special attention to any text features. For example, bolded, italicized, or underlined words are likely to be important to the task. Make use of the highlighter and notepad in your universal tools to take notes that will help you identify important parts of the text. Remember, you might be asked to watch a video or look at a picture instead of reading a text. In that case, pay careful attention to what is said or what is shown because you will likely be asked to recall and analyze these non-text items when you answer the task and questions at hand.

3. Reread the Questions and Narrow Down the Answer Choices

Once you've reread the questions, complete any easy ones first. Note any key words or important ideas. Eliminate any distracters or obviously wrong answer choices. If you cannot eliminate any choices, then take a guess. If you aren't certain of your guess, mark the question for review and return to it later.

Practice Exercises

Now practice what you've learned about these technology-enhanced tasks. Since this is a physical book, not a computer, we have modified the language of the questions a bit. For example, for a task that would ask you to "click" on something in the stimulus material, we may ask you to circle that item or draw a line underneath it. For a task that would ask you to drag-and-drop an item from one location to another, we may ask you to rewrite the correct order of items on scratch paper. By practicing these questions, you will get a sense of how they will be formatted and what they will be asking.

While you do not have access to all the universal tools, you can mimic several of them. Highlight and annotate the text. Take notes on a separate sheet of paper, if you need to. Cross out eliminated answer choices. For each task, orient yourself first, and then read the stimulus text carefully. Finally, reread the tasks and questions and eliminate answer choices. The correct answers and explanations can be found in Chapter 6.

Exercise 1

College and Career Readiness Anchor Standard for Reading R.1

Read closely to determine what the text says explicitly and to make logical inferences from it; cite specific textual evidence when writing or speaking to support conclusions drawn from the text.

College and Career Readiness Anchor Standard for Reading R.3

Analyze how and why individuals, events, or ideas develop and interact over the course of a text.

College and Career Readiness Anchor Standard for Reading R.5

Analyze the structure of texts, including how specific sentences, paragraphs, and larger portions of the text (e.g., a section, chapter, scene, or stanza) relate to each other and the whole.

Common Core Standard W.8.5

With some guidance and support from peers and adults, develop and strengthen writing as needed by planning, revising, editing, rewriting, or trying a new approach, focusing on how well purpose and audience have been addressed.

Common Core Standard L.8.4.A

Use context (e.g., the overall meaning of a sentence or paragraph; a word's position or function in a sentence) as a clue to the meaning of a word or phrase.

 **HELPFUL HINT**

Remember, you must respond to all tasks in a section before you can move on to the next section.

Directions: Read the following passage, and complete questions 1 and 2.

Franklin is the coach of the baseball team at Washington Middle School. He was frustrated that his team had lost the first five games of the season. Franklin wanted to analyze why his team was struggling. First, he listed the game's several parts: pitching, batting, fielding, and base running. Then, he thought carefully about how his team was handling these aspects.

He realized the team was doing very well with offense. The team was batting and base running well. However, he realized that they were having a hard time with defense. The fielders were doing a great job, but the pitchers were struggling. As a result, the other teams were hitting too many pitches and scoring. Poor pitching was the <u>dominant</u> problem for the team. Franklin decided to recruit a new pitcher and coached the other pitchers on some pitching techniques. Once these steps were taken, the team won all of the remaining games in the season.

1. What is the best synonym for the underlined word in the passage?

  ○ A. sleepy
  ○ B. common
  ○ C. central
  ○ D. minor

 **HELPFUL HINT**

On the computerized test, a question like question 1 would ask you to click on the word "dominant," which would then unlock a drop-down menu of potential synonyms to choose from. You would then click on your answer selection.

2. Arrange the following events in chronological order. Write your answer in the box below.

Franklin examined the connections, or relationships, among the parts.

Franklin listed the features of these parts.

Franklin made a new plan.

Franklin divided the thing or idea into its parts.

Franklin examined the connections, or relationships, between each part and the whole.

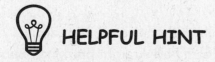 **HELPFUL HINT**

On the computerized test, question 2 would be a drag-and-drop question. You would use your mouse to click and drag the events into chronological order.

(Answers are on page 150.)

Exercise 2

Common Core Standard W.8.3.D

Use precise words and phrases, relevant descriptive details, and sensory language to capture the action and convey experiences and events.

Common Core Standard L.8.1

Demonstrate command of the conventions of standard English grammar and usage when writing or speaking.

Directions: Read each paragraph, and complete the task that accompanies it.

 HELPFUL HINT

For both tasks in this exercise, on the computerized test, you would click on the sections of each paragraph that the question asks you to circle.

1. The movie I saw yesterday was OK! Even though it was a drama, it had many hysterical moments. The main characters drove the plot with such extreme force that I forgot they were famous actors who I knew from previous films. In certain moments, I felt so nervous—my heart often raced until the writers would insert a joke to break the tension. One time, I scattered my popcorn on the person next to me when I jumped. Even the music was nice. I hope the entire cast will reassemble for a sequel.

    Circle the two adjectives from the paragraph that should be replaced with more precise descriptive words.

2. Sarah loved to play with an old, filthy doll. She received it from her grandmother when she was five-years-old. It had straight black hair Sarah named the doll Maria. After her grandmother. Sarah traveled everywhere with Maria, which had soiled the doll considerably. Washing the doll would be very challenged because of how fragile the doll had become.

    Circle all the sentences that do *not* have any errors in grammar, usage, or mechanics.

(Answers are on page 152.)

Exercise 3

College and Career Readiness Anchor Standard for Reading R.10

Read and comprehend complex literary and informational texts independently and proficiently.

College and Career Readiness Anchor Standard for Language L.5

Demonstrate understanding of figurative language, word relationships, and nuances in word meanings.

Common Core Standard RL.8.2

Determine a theme or central idea of a text and analyze its development over the course of the text, including its relationship to the characters, setting, and plot; provide an objective summary of the text.

Common Core Standard RL.8.10

By the end of the year, read and comprehend literature, including stories, dramas, and poems, at the high end of grades 6–8 text complexity band independently and proficiently.

Directions: Below is a poem in which the speaker discusses her feelings about a relationship. Read the poem, and answer questions 1 and 2.

A Bird Came Down the Walk (328)

by Emily Dickinson

In the Garden

A bird came down the walk:
He did not know I saw;
He bit an angle-worm in halves
And ate the fellow, raw.

And then he drank a dew
From a convenient grass,
And then hopped sidewise to the wall
To let a beetle pass.

He glanced with rapid eyes
That hurried all abroad,—
They looked like frightened beads, I thought;
He stirred his velvet head

Like one in danger; cautious,
I offered him a crumb,
And he unrolled his feathers
And rowed him softer home

Than oars divide the ocean,
Too silver for a seam,
Or butterflies, off banks of noon,
Leap, plashless, as they swim.

1. Check off all of the poetic devices used in this poem from the list below.

   ☐ metaphor

   ☐ allegory

   ☐ simile

   ☐ personification

   ☐ hyperbole

   ☐ alliteration

   HELPFUL HINT

   On the computerized test, for question 1, you would use your mouse to click on each correct poetic device from the list.

2. Circle the line or lines from the poem that best illustrate the climax of the poem.

   HELPFUL HINT

   On the computerized test, for question 2, you would click on the line or lines from the poem that best illustrate the climax of the poem.

(Answers are on page 152.)

Constructed-Response Tasks

CHAPTER 3

Overview

The constructed-response tasks require you to construct a brief written response after reviewing and analyzing a stimulus text or a non-text item. The text could be from any genre, and it could be fiction or nonfiction. You may also be asked to examine a non-text item, such as a picture or a video clip. Usually, you will be required to review a text and look for something specific (e.g., a theme or a central idea). Then you will be prompted to write a short response that discusses the text you analyzed by using textual evidence and reasoning, or you might be required to revise the text. You may also be asked to write an ending to a text or any number of responses to it.

In most instances, you will need to write either an **explanation**, an **argument**, or a **narrative** (a story). Expect to see all three types of responses at some point during the test. In your responses to these tasks, the test makers expect you to demonstrate a clear, insightful understanding of the text or non-text item *and* create a thoughtful written response. Approximately thirty to forty percent of the test will require constructed responses. The scoring for these questions uses a tiered two-point system based on specific criteria for that question. See Table I-2 on page 5 for a Sample Scoring Rubric for a Constructed-Response Task, but remember that each question has its own specific grading criteria.

Like selected-response tasks and technology-enhanced tasks, each constructed-response task has three parts, although they are not labeled. The first part will provide context for the stimulus text or non-text item and directions for completing the task at hand. It will likely provide the purpose of the writing. The stimulus text or non-text item is the second part. Often, the stimulus will be incomplete in some way, and you will be asked to complete it. The last part is the prompt. It will have a target statement that will ask you to do something very specific (i.e., "write a conclusion for…," or "add evidence to the second paragraph to support the claim…"). The stimulus will likely be used to answer a few selected-response tasks or technology-enhanced tasks in addition to the constructed-response tasks.

There are many prompt possibilities, and they can be simple or quite complex. You may be asked to revise a section or complete the text. You may be asked to analyze some aspect of literature (e.g., mood, image, theme, etc.) or an aspect of the author's argument. Sometimes, you may be provided with some "student notes" that you must use to complete a paragraph. Very often, you will be required to give very specific textual evidence or examples to support your writing. Expect to write several sentences and up to several paragraphs depending on the task in response to each of the constructed-response prompts.

Strategies

1. Orientation

Read the overview and the prompts carefully first (skipping the stimulus text or non-text item for now). By understanding the prompts first, you can be a more effective reader. Look for key words that will tell you exactly what to look for when reading the stimulus material. Use the highlighter tool to mark the key words, and use your notepad tool to start jotting down ideas for a response. Below is a list of common verbs, followed by a list of common nouns on page 43, that will likely be used for constructed-response questions and tasks. Be sure that you are familiar with the meaning of each word.

Verbs			
analyze	define	explain	respond
apply	demonstrate	identify	retell
argue	describe	illustrate	revise
articulate	determine	infer	state
cite	develop	integrate	suggest
click	discuss	interpret	summarize
compare	distinguish	justify	support
compose	edit	locate	synthesize
contrast	evaluate	persuade	trace
critique	examine	predict	

Nouns		
adjective	evidence	point of view
analogy	explanation	rhetoric
argument	figurative language	simile
cause (and effect)	illustration	stanza
central idea	interaction	structure
claim	metaphor	theme
connection	mood	tone
details	narrative	

2. Read the Stimulus Material

Read the stimulus material carefully. Use your universal tools to expand the text to help focus on the reading passage specifically. Pay special attention to any text features. For example, bolded, italicized, or underlined words are likely to be important to the task. Make use of the highlighter and notepad in your universal tools to take notes that will help you identify important parts of the text. Be sure to identify evidence and examples that will help you complete the task.

3. Reread the Prompt

Determine what sort of response the prompt is asking for. Is it looking for an explanation, an argument, or a narrative? Are you revising or completing the text? Are you providing an analysis? Identify exactly what the task is asking you to do. Be sure to note any specific information you will need to include in your response. No matter what you are asked to write, you will be assessed on your ability to write clearly with accurate spelling, proper grammar usage, and correct conventions.

4. Construct Your Response

Using the notepad, quickly outline your response. Whenever possible, you should include textual evidence or examples, so list key ideas or textual evidence that you would like to use. Precise details and quotes from the stimulus material will best support your response. Whenever you quote direct text, you must use quotation marks and cite the source. When paraphrasing, you do not need to use quotation marks, but you must still cite your source.

Crafting a Paragraph

No matter what sort of response is required (explanation, argument, or narrative), there are some basic paragraph elements that you will be required to include in any type of response. The **topic sentence** announces what you will be discussing in the paragraph. This will help you maintain focus in the paragraph. Be sure to use **sign posts**, a type of transition word, to introduce each point you are making within the paragraph. Announcing things in numerical order often helps the reader track your ideas. For example:

There are three ways of...

The first way to...

Another way to...

The last way to...

The author makes two points...

The primary point...

Secondly, the author states...

These types of sign posts are not appropriate in every type of writing. You will still need **transition words** to help the reader follow your writing. The list on page 45 is just a starter list of transition words and phrases; there are many, many more ways of doing this. When completing the practice exercises in this chapter, try using a few of these to help relate the sequence of events in your written response.

Transition Words

above all	for this reason	likewise
after all	from	near
all of a sudden	further	not only ... but
alongside	generally speaking	not to mention
although	given that	notably
another key point	here	obviously
as well as	however	of course
beyond	important to realize	regardless
by and large	in case	sooner or later
consequently	in effect	surprisingly
coupled with	in order to	then again
despite	in the beginning	there
especially	in the distance	to clarify
even though	in the first place	to say nothing of
eventually	in the hope that	whenever
finally	in the long run	with this in mind
for example	including	
for instance	instantly	

Preparing to Write Narrative Responses

You will be scored on how well you write your story. You may be asked to write an ending to an existing story, rewrite one of the paragraphs from the original text, or write some other portion of the story. Keep in mind the plot, the characters, and the setting, and be sure to use many details because they will be expected. Make sure that you are continuing with the existing elements of the story; it is very unlikely that you will be asked to write something from scratch. More than likely, the prompt will ask you to expand or extend something in the stimulus text.

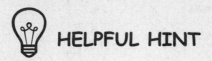

HELPFUL HINT

Keep in mind the point of view! If the given stimulus text is written in the first-person point of view (using pronouns like "I," "me," and "you" in the narration), the test graders expect that you will continue with that point of view. Don't suddenly switch to a third-person point of view (using pronouns like "he," "she," and "they").

Preparing to Write Explanative and Argumentative Responses

Be sure to include two to four pieces of evidence per paragraph. Evidence can be in the form of a quotation from the stimulus text, a fact or data from the stimulus text, or an example from the stimulus material (even a personal example). Table 3-1 discusses the various types of evidence in greater detail.

Table 3-1. Types of Evidence

Quotations	Facts or Data	Examples
> Use the exact words from the stimulus text. > Be sure to use correct citation punctuation. > Be sure to credit the source.	> Facts and data include names, dates, number comparisons, etc. > Be sure to credit the source.	> Examples include observations from the sources provided (sometimes this includes non-text items such as a video, a picture, a chart, or a comic). > Examples can be personal. > Examples can be hypothetical. > Be sure to credit the source even when you are not directly quoting but are still paraphrasing. > Only use personal and hypothetical examples in addition to other types of evidence cited from the stimulus text. Do not rely on personal and hypothetical examples alone.

Each of these types of evidence needs a lead-in, a proper citation, a restatement, and an explanation that reinforces your claim. Table 3-2 illustrates how to accomplish all of these goals.

Table 3-2. How to Introduce Evidence in Your Writing

Evidence and Elaboration Parts	What Do I Write?	How Much Do I Write?	Example
Lead-in	> Give context for the evidence. > Give the name of the author or the title of the text, if appropriate.	1 complete sentence or a part of the sentence that leads into the evidence itself	The National Safety Council published information to help parents understand the health problems that many students face, especially when it comes to carrying around a backpack.
Evidence	> Evidence consists of quotations, facts or data, and/or examples. > Always cite the source.	The length of the actual quotation and proper citation varies, but use the least amount possible. Be sure to cut straight to the point. Don't include quotes that do not support your argument, and keep the citations as concise as possible.	The American Chiropractic Association urges that "... a full backpack weigh no more than 10 percent of a child's weight." ("Backpack Safety: It's Time to Lighten the Load") or According to "Backpack Safety: It's Time to Lighten the Load," an article published by the National Safety Council with recommendations from the American Chiropractic Association, a backpack should weigh no more than ten percent of a child's weight.
Restatement (What this means is ...)	> Restate the evidence in *your own words*, even if it feels repetitive.	1 complete sentence is usually sufficient	In other words, if a student weighs eighty pounds, his backpack shouldn't weigh more than eight pounds.
Tie back to your claim/point/ commentary (Why this matters ...)	> Explain how the evidence supports your claim/point/ commentary (i.e., "This means ..." or "This is an example of ..." or "This shows ...")	2 or 3 complete sentences are usually necessary	A science textbook and a multiple-section binder can easily total eight pounds, so if a student carries around all of his books all day it will certainly affect his health.

Each paragraph should have a **topic sentence**. The topic sentence announces what the paragraph is going to be about. Your topic sentence should be followed by several supporting sentences full of details from the text. For example, read the following stimulus text followed by the constructed-response prompt and the sample low-scoring and high-scoring student responses to this prompt.

Ed Ricketts ran his marine biology lab on Cannery Row in Monterey, which was very close to where John Steinbeck was living at the time, and Steinbeck would stop by to help in the lab and also to talk with Ricketts. They found they both had an insatiable curiosity about most things and were like-minded. Both men's marriages fell apart, and, as a result of this they looked after each other. Ricketts brought Steinbeck on multiple scientific explorations in the Gulf of Mexico. Both he and Steinbeck wrote about these adventures, but without much success. On May 8, 1948, Ricketts was involved in a terrible car accident that killed him several days later. Steinbeck was crushed and fell into a deep depression as a result.

Constructed-Response Prompt: Explain why Steinbeck fell into a deep depression. Use details from the text to support your answer.

Sample Low-Scoring Student Response

Steinbeck was depressed about the death of his friend.

(Notice that this response only addresses the prompt as briefly as possible. It does not cite any evidence from the text.)

Sample High-Scoring Student Response

Steinbeck was depressed about the death of his friend. He and Ricketts had developed a close friendship, "looking after each other" after both of their marriages fell apart. As a result, they relied on one another for company. Since they were so like-minded, they spent time completing "multiple scientific explorations" and subsequently wrote about these adventures. Since he depended so heavily on his friend, Steinbeck was shocked and greatly saddened when Ricketts died.

(Notice that this response not only addresses the prompt, but it also cites specific details from the text that support the argument that Steinbeck fell into a depression because of the death of his close friend. The closing sentence also helps finish and complete the paragraph.)

Practice Exercises

Exercise 1—Narrative Response

College and Career Readiness Anchor Standard for Writing W.3

Write narratives to develop real or imagined experiences or events using effective technique, well-chosen details, and well-structured event sequences.

College and Career Readiness Anchor Standard for Language L.1

Demonstrate command of the conventions of standard English grammar and usage when writing or speaking.

College and Career Readiness Anchor Standard for Language L.2

Demonstrate command of the conventions of standard English capitalization, punctuation, and spelling when writing.

Common Core Standard RL.8.2

Determine a theme or central idea of a text and analyze its development over the course of the text, including its relationship to the characters, setting, and plot; provide an objective summary of the text.

Common Core Standard RL.8.4

Determine the meaning of words and phrases as they are used in a text, including figurative and connotative meanings; analyze the impact of specific word choices on meaning and tone, including analogies or allusions to other texts.

Common Core Standard W.8.3

Write narratives to develop real or imagined experiences of events using effective technique, relevant descriptive details, and well-constructed event sequences.

Common Core Standard W.8.3.D

Use precise words and phrases, relevant descriptive details, and sensory language to capture the action and convey experiences and events.

 HELPFUL HINT

Don't forget, you must respond to all tasks in a section before you can move on to the next section.

Directions: Samantha is writing a narrative about her memories of her mother and her mother's cookbook. Read her description below, and complete the task that follows.

As I took my mother's cookbook from the shelf, several yellowed recipe cards fluttered to the floor. The tattered spine of the cookbook was worn through so that I could feel the binding in my hand. It smelled of birthday cakes, soups, and pot roasts—my childhood.

Continue this description of Samantha's story of cooking with her mother when she was a child. Use vivid details about sights, sounds, smells, and/or feelings that will fully develop this paragraph. Write your response in the box below. Sample responses can be found beginning on page 153.

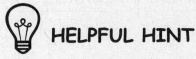 HELPFUL HINT

On the computerized test, you would be typing your responses to all of the constructed-response tasks. Be sure to practice your typing skills so that you can type your responses as clearly as possible with ease.

Exercise 2—Explanatory Response

College and Career Readiness Anchor Standard for Reading R.1

Read closely to determine what the text says explicitly and to make logical inferences from it; cite specific textual evidence when writing or speaking to support conclusions drawn from the text.

College and Career Readiness Anchor Standard for Reading R.2

Determine central ideas or themes of a text and analyze their development; summarize the key supporting details and ideas.

College and Career Readiness Anchor Standard for Writing W.2

Write informative/explanatory texts to examine and convey complex ideas and information clearly and accurately through the effective selection, organization, and analysis of content.

College and Career Readiness Anchor Standard for Language L.1

Demonstrate command of the conventions of standard English grammar and usage when writing or speaking.

College and Career Readiness Anchor Standard for Language L.2

Demonstrate command of the conventions of standard English capitalization, punctuation, and spelling when writing.

Common Core Standard RI.8.2

Determine a central idea of a text and analyze its development over the course of the text, including its relationship to supporting ideas; provide an objective summary of the text.

Common Core Standard W.8.1.E

Provide a concluding statement or section that follows from and supports the argument presented.

Directions: A student is writing a biography of the American author John Steinbeck. Read the beginning of that biography below, and complete the task that follows.

Never at Peace: A Brief Biography of John Steinbeck

John Steinbeck is one of the most famous American writers. He was born in 1902 in Salinas, California. He and his sisters grew up with modest means, as his father was a bookkeeper and his mother, Olive Hamilton, was a former school teacher. She was the one who likely fostered Steinbeck's love of reading and writing. One of his favorite books to read as a child was *Le Morte d'Arthur* by Sir Thomas Malory, which is a collection of stories about King Arthur. He and his sisters loved to play "King Arthur" in the nearby Castle Rock Park. When Steinbeck was fourteen, he decided to become a writer. He was smart and very shy, and he often locked himself in his room to write stories and poems. He loved anything mechanical and could often be found repairing things. Another early influence on Steinbeck's writing was his high school English teacher, who strongly encouraged Steinbeck to write. During his summers while in high school, he worked at Spreckels' sugar beet farms, both in the fields and in the factory laboratory. Working in the fields would strongly influence his writing later on.

John Steinbeck graduated from Salinas High School in 1919 and started Stanford University, in California, that same fall. He frequently took jobs working on California farms to help pay for schooling and also because he didn't like college very much. Eventually he dropped out without earning a degree in 1925. He moved to New York City and tried to work as a freelance writer, but he was not very successful, and he eventually moved back to California.

Working in the fields paid off in many ways for John Steinbeck. The farms were full of migrant farm workers, and their stories fascinated him. He wrote several short stories, but his first successful novel was *Tortilla Flat* (1935). This was a humorous story about Salinas Valley farmers. His next novel, called *In Dubious Battle* (1936), was much more serious, depicting the struggles of migrant fruit pickers. One of his more famous novels, *Of Mice and Men* (1937), also tells the story of California farmers. While writing these novels, Steinbeck wrote articles for the *San Francisco Chronicle* newspaper to earn extra money.

After researching and writing several heartbreaking articles about migrant farm workers in California, he collected this research and turned it into one of his most famous works, *The Grapes of Wrath* (1939), which eventually helped him win the Nobel Prize in Literature in 1962. This launched him into fame. He struggled with his fame, as he was so very shy and being recognizable made him uncomfortable. He also felt tremendous pressure from the public to write another incredible book. Additionally, Steinbeck's marriage wasn't doing well. Even with his writing success, he was miserable.

During this time, John Steinbeck did, however, make a strong friend in marine biologist Ed Ricketts. Like Steinbeck, Ricketts had also dropped out of college and never received a degree from the University of Chicago. Ed Ricketts ran his marine biology lab on Cannery Row in Monterey, which was very close to where John Steinbeck was living at the time, and Steinbeck would stop by to help in the lab and also to talk with Ricketts. They found they both had an insatiable curiosity about most things and were like-minded. Both men's marriages fell apart, and as a result of this they looked after each other. Ricketts brought Steinbeck on multiple scientific explorations in the Gulf of Mexico. Both he and Steinbeck wrote about these adventures, but without much success. On May 8, 1948, Ricketts was involved in a terrible car accident that killed him several days later. Steinbeck was crushed and fell into a deep depression as a result.

Student Notes for Conclusion	> He wrote *East of Eden* in 1952 (famous book). > He wrote *Travels with Charley* in 1962 (famous book). > Steinbeck died in 1968. > He wrote dozens of fiction and nonfiction books. > His books are read in schools all over the world.

Using the student notes provided, write a conclusion for this biography. Write your response in the box below. Sample responses can be found beginning on page 154.

Exercise 3—Argumentative Response

College and Career Readiness Anchor Standard for Reading R.1

Read closely to determine what the text says explicitly and to make logical inferences from it; cite specific textual evidence when writing or speaking to support conclusions drawn from the text.

College and Career Readiness Anchor Standard for Reading R.2

Determine central ideas or themes of a text and analyze their development; summarize the key supporting details and ideas.

College and Career Readiness Anchor Standard for Reading R.8

Delineate and evaluate the argument and specific claims in a text, including the validity of the reasoning as well as the relevance and sufficiency of the evidence.

College and Career Readiness Anchor Standard for Reading R.9

Analyze how two or more texts address similar themes or topics in order to build knowledge or to compare the approaches the authors take.

College and Career Readiness Anchor Standard for Writing W.1

Write arguments to support claims in an analysis of substantive topics or texts using valid reasoning and relevant and sufficient evidence.

College and Career Readiness Anchor Standard for Writing W.9

Draw evidence from literary or informational texts to support analysis, reflection, and research.

College and Career Readiness Anchor Standard for Language L.1

Demonstrate command of the conventions of standard English grammar and usage when writing or speaking.

College and Career Readiness Anchor Standard for Language L.2

Demonstrate command of the conventions of standard English capitalization, punctuation, and spelling when writing.

Common Core Standard RI.8.1

Cite textual evidence that most strongly supports an analysis of what the text says explicitly as well as inferences drawn from the text.

Common Core Standard W.8.1

Write arguments to support claims with clear reasons and relevant evidence.

Common Core Standard W.8.1.A

Introduce claim(s), acknowledge and distinguish the claim(s) from alternative or opposing claims, and organize the reasons and evidence logically.

Common Core Standard W.8.1.B

Support claim(s) with logical reasoning and relevant evidence, using accurate, credible sources and demonstrating an understanding of the topic or text.

Directions: Using technology in friendships is controversial. Read Sofia's and Felipe's arguments below, and complete the task that follows.

Is One Type of Friendship Better Than the Other?

Most teenagers in America are socializing online in addition to hanging out with friends at school. Is one way better than the other? We asked two students to weigh in with their opinions.

Sofia: Technology enhances friendships more than ever before.

Let's face it; you can't be everywhere all the time. Teens are pulled in many directions at once. They have to spend time with their families, doing their homework, competing in sports, and participating in clubs. Who can hang out with friends in person all the time? Friends can't always be with you. Teens want to support others and be supported, and this is next to impossible in the evenings or on weekends without digital assistance. Even before smartphones, teens were on old-fashioned telephones chatting for hours. Fast texts, tweets, and instant messages allow us to connect quickly without having to meet up. That can be crucial when freaking out about an upcoming math test or after having a fight with your sister, and you need a little support. Getting a text or a "like" feels good because someone took the time to understand and respond directly to you. Technology allows us to be freer with one another without in-person cliques or squad pressures to say the right thing. You can also talk with people from different friend circles at the same time without the awkwardness of radically different people trying to get along. Sometimes a school or neighborhood can be limiting.

Online, teens can connect to people with similar interests that might not be available at school or home. Meeting friends through fan pages or in an online game feels very accepting when others at home don't share the same interests. Meeting friends online can open up the doors to meeting in person, too, which might not have happened otherwise. Shy or introverted people can cautiously approach a new friendship online instead of having to put themselves on the spot in front of a crowd of judgmental people. Technology is making friendships stronger.

Felipe: There is no substitute for in-person friendships.

Fully learning about somebody through a screen is impossible. Everyone knows that people play roles and aren't completely honest when they are online or texting. It's like a masquerade ball, where everyone is wearing a mask so they can act differently from how they are in real life. People edit their true selves to be more fantastic than who they really are. For instance, people only post flattering pictures of themselves, even if the same picture is not flattering to their friends. Teens aren't completely truthful online. Besides leaving out parts, the whole truth can be distorted in other ways, too. People can exaggerate or outright lie very easily, so a person can never be sure who he or she is dealing with. It can actually be quite dangerous as there are people who are predatory online. In addition, there is so much drama when messages are misinterpreted. Everyone has experienced writing a text or comment and the other person misunderstands the tone or context. Teens love sarcasm, and this is the hardest thing to get right in texts, which can cause many fights and hurt feelings. Friends block and dump each other too quickly instead of being forced to work things out, which creates an unstable foundation for friendships that could be toppled at any moment by one misunderstood sarcastic tweet. Aside from protecting oneself or existing friendships, teens should spend more time together because there is nothing like joking around and hanging out with your friends. The body language of goofy faces and laughter cannot be properly mimicked by electronics. Think of all the experiences you can never fully share through a screen, like going for a hike or sharing a meal together. A huge percentage of human communication happens through body language and cannot happen using a smartphone or a computer. There have been plenty of studies that have shown that the human touch is actually healing. A text is not a substitute for a hug when your best friend is feeling down. Think about it, would you rather see your friend's face or a smiley face emoji?

Using the arguments from "Is One Type of Friendship Better Than the Other?" write a paragraph in which you argue whether you think technology helps or hurts teens' friendships. Write your response in the box below. Sample responses can be found beginning on page 155.

CHAPTER 4

Performance Task Overview

Overview

The Performance Task is meant to simulate real classroom learning and writing experiences. It consists of two sessions. The first is the lesson, and the second is the actual task itself.

Think of the first session as an information-gathering session. Typically, an instructor will discuss a topic and have the class brainstorm more information on the topic, which normally takes about 30 minutes. This is your opportunity to ask any questions you may have about the topic on which you will be writing. Nothing in this session is scored. Any notes or work that you write down will not be allowed into the second session. This first session is really just a relaxed opportunity to become familiar with the topic in a traditional classroom setting, giving you a chance to talk to the instructor and to hear other students discuss the topic.

The second session is divided into two parts: reading and writing. You will be given several sources to examine, which could include a video, a chart, a graph, a picture, a fiction or nonfiction text, or a poem. Then, you will be asked to complete a few constructed-response questions about the reading. (For more on constructed-response questions, review Chapter 3.) Finally, you will be asked to write one of the following: an **argumentative or explanatory essay**, or a short **real or imagined narrative**. While this session is not timed, it usually takes at least 70 to 120 minutes to complete.

The prompt that you will be given in the second session determines which of the two types of essays you will write. If you follow the directions closely, answering all parts of the prompt, you will automatically write the correct type of essay. If you are nervous about what to write, review the prompt and then ask yourself, "Do I have to write an essay or a narrative?" The prompt should clearly have the key words "essay" or "narrative." Once you have figured out what the prompt is asking you to write, you can plan your writing.

A narrative tells a story, but what is the difference between an explanatory essay and an argumentative essay? It's important to be able to know the similarities and differences between these two essay types so that you can make the most out of your response. Table 4-1 outlines these two types of essays.

Table 4-1. Explanatory Essays vs. Argumentative Essays

Explanatory Essay	> Investigate a topic. > Collect, generate, and evaluate evidence. > Then present **other peoples' opinions** on the topic. > It explains another person's information in detail and explains what is difficult to understand. Note that there could be more than two sides of an issue though you do not have to address all of the sides of the issue.
Argumentative Essay	> Investigate a topic. > Collect, generate, and evaluate evidence. > Then establish **your position** on the topic in a concise manner. Usually, there are only two sides of the issue. Explain what both sides are, but then take one side and provide a **counterargument** and a rebuttal.

Your response will be scored in these three areas—**organization**, **evidence/ elaboration**, and **conventions**. Note that the **argumentative** essay requires the extra **counterargument**. Accidentally including a counterargument in an explanatory essay won't hurt your score, even if you do not identify the genre correctly, but you need a counterargument to achieve the highest score for the argumentative essay.

Scoring

To maximize your points on this section of the test, your writing should include:

1. The **statement of purpose** or "focus" score is going to evaluate how well you make a claim and stick to the topic. Most importantly, you must have a clear thesis statement and clear topic sentences for each body paragraph.

2. You will be scored higher if you **organize** the essay into purposeful paragraphs. You must have an **introductory paragraph**, **several body paragraphs** (two to four is preferable), and a **conclusion paragraph**. It is

critical that you organize your essay well since good organization affects all areas of scoring.

3. Graders will also be looking for **transitions and phrases**. You need to be able to use clear transitions between ideas.

4. For the argumentative essay only, you will also need to provide a **counterargument**. You will be evaluated on your ability to acknowledge and address opposing arguments through a counterargument. Supporting your claim well requires that you select **relevant evidence** from your sources and **elaborate** on this evidence. This is done in the body paragraphs.

5. Finally, you will be scored based on your **grammar**, **punctuation**, **capitalization**, and **spelling**. You are allowed to make a few mistakes (but not a lot), as long as the mistakes do not deter the meaning of your writing.

Argumentative or Explanatory Essay Strategies

These strategies will help you write either an argumentative essay or an explanatory essay. The type of prompt should help you determine which of these two types of essays you are being asked to write. To provide you with a clear example of how to follow the strategies for writing an argumentative essay or an explanatory essay, throughout this section, we will refer to the full "Backpacks Performance Task" starting on page 85.

1. Orientation

Read the task and the directions. Ask yourself:

> * What is the topic?
> * What are the sources?
> * What does the prompt ask me to write?

Asking yourself these questions will give you an idea of where you are heading and whether you are going to be writing a narrative or an essay. Review the task and directions for the "Backpacks Performance Task," reprinted on page 62, and determine whether you will be writing a narrative or an essay.

BACKPACKS PERFORMANCE TASK

Task:

Students may be in physical danger simply by carrying a heavy backpack, which can lead to serious health effects. However, many students believe backpacks help with organization. Some schools have responded by providing lockers for storage, but this might not be the answer either.

Should students be allowed to bring their backpacks to class? This is the subject of the article you will be writing for your school newspaper. In your research, you have come across three helpful sources arguing various angles of this debate.

In Part 1, you will carefully review these sources, and then you will answer some questions. Briefly scan the sources and the three questions that follow. In Part 2, you will write an argumentative essay on whether students should be allowed to bring their backpacks to class.

Directions:

1. Read all the sources, and take notes.

2. Answer three questions about the sources.

3. Plan and write your essay.

After reading this task, you probably noticed the central idea: *Should students be allowed to bring their backpacks to class?* You probably also noticed that you are expected to write an *argumentative essay* that would fit into the *school newspaper*. You know what you are writing, and you also know who the audience is.

2. Examine the Sources

The test makers will supply a few sources that will provide a wide view of a topic. Sometimes, the sources will share the same view; other times they will present opposing points of view. You will likely find one source more useful to cite than the others, but you should attempt to use all of them in some way. During this process, it is essential that you take notes and highlight relevant information. Scan each source, looking at the titles, any graphics, or any other interesting information. If you are given a video or a picture, you should also refer to it in your writing. You can rewatch videos to get an exact quotation, and you should reference videos by time (e.g., *At 3:29 minutes, Ms. Miller says…*). Try to cluster or group notes on the global notes, which will help you write an outline later. Table 4-2 presents a quick table that you could write as part of your notes when reviewing this Performance Task.

Table 4-2. Taking Notes for the Performance Task

Issue	Pro Arguments	Con Arguments
Should students be allowed to bring their backpacks to class?	> Organization > Accessibility > Lockers are not safe	> Back and shoulder injuries > Classroom theft > Tripping hazard

Fully examine the sources, but also manage your time so you won't be rushed when writing your response. Look at the time remaining, and budget how much time you will need to plan, write, and revise your essay. While you do have unlimited time, if you need more time than that allotted, your testing administrator may need to move you to another location to complete the test.

3. Respond to the Constructed-Response Tasks

There are usually three constructed-response tasks, and they will be scored in addition to the essay. Be specific, give examples from the sources, and include details. Use the same strategies discussed in Chapter 3 regarding constructed-response tasks. Page 64 contains a sample constructed-response task for this Performance Task followed by a sample low-scoring student response and a sample high-scoring student response.

Constructed-Response Task: What is the main issue that students using backpacks face? Use details from the sources to support your answer.

Sample Low-Scoring Student Response

Students experience health issues.

Sample High-Scoring Student Response

Students experience "back and shoulder pain, and poor posture" because their backpacks are too heavy.

(Notice that this response includes specific details from a source to support the claim.)

4. Write Your Two-Part Claim (Thesis Statement)

Review the task, and write your claim, which shows the reader your ideas. Use language directly from the task to help guide your statement. Questions can be flipped around to help make statements that include your claim.

Question: *Should students be allowed to bring their backpacks to class?*

Claim: *Students should not be allowed to bring their backpacks to class because…*

Often, scope is an overlooked portion of the claim. The **scope** tells the reader how much of the topic you will be discussing, somewhat like a frame around a picture. State specifically what you are going to discuss in your essay. For example, if you were asked what your favorite ice cream flavor is and you wrote, "vanilla is best," you would have left out scope. What are you referring to when you say "vanilla"? Do you mean vanilla cookies? What about vanilla air fresheners? Instead, write something specific like, "I prefer vanilla ice cream." This clearer statement provides the reader with a clear range of what is being discussed and the exact scope of your idea. Take a look at the sample claim below, and see if you can figure out what the topic and scope are and what the claim/stand is.

Claim Example: *Students should not be allowed to bring backpacks to class because they cause health issues, create safety problems, and distract students from paying attention in class.*

Topic and Scope: The topic and scope state what you will be discussing and how much of the topic you will be discussing. In this case, the topic is "whether or not students should be allowed to bring backpacks to class." We know that the writer will be talking about student backpacks and is only going to focus on whether or not they should be brought to class. "Class" is the scope. The writer is only concerned with whether backpacks are appropriate for the classroom. The writer is not concerned with whether backpacks are safe in any situation, such as when riding a bicycle. The only matter at hand is whether they are safe for class.

Claim/Stand: The claim/stand presents your argument regarding the issue at hand. It tells the reader what side you are on. In this case, the phrase "should not" signifies your claim that students should not be allowed to bring backpacks to class, and the rest of the sentence provides supporting details to back up your claim. If you aren't sure how to state your claim, think what someone else would write if he were to disagree with your point of view. For example, a counterargument might be:

Counterargument: *Students should be allowed to bring their backpacks to class because they help students stay organized, get to class on time, and protect their belongings.*

Clearly, if there are several reasons why a person may argue in favor of using backpacks in class, then you need to strongly state that you are opposed to this and why you feel it is an unsafe practice.

Supporting Details: These are a summary of support that will be used in your essay to support your claim. In the original example, the supporting details are "cause health issues, create safety problems, and distract students from paying attention in class." These are the three reasons given in support of banning backpacks in class. Each of these reasons should be addressed in its own paragraph, and each reason could also be shaped into a topic sentence for its respective body paragraph. For example, when discussing the fact that backpacks in class "cause health issues," a suitable topic sentence would be "Students should not bring backpacks to class because they cause a number of health issues."

Keep in mind that, when writing your essay, you will need to include your claim in both your introduction and your conclusion. Restating the claim in a fresh way can sometimes be tricky. If you get stuck, try inverting the claim statement by flipping the end and the beginning around.

Claim in the Introduction: *Students should not be allowed to bring backpacks to class because they cause health issues, create safety problems, and distract students from paying attention in class.*

Claim in the Conclusion: *Since backpacks cause health issues, create safety problems, and distract students from paying attention in class, they should not be allowed in classrooms.*

5. Create Your Outline

Use your claim to create an outline. Too many students don't fully outline their essay and rush on to the first draft too quickly, mistakenly thinking that creating an outline is a waste of time when they could be writing. As a result, it is very possible that they will leave out important information or go off topic. **Take the time to outline properly**. You are likely to find that creating an outline and developing a thesis statement happen at the same time since they are so closely linked.

Creating a proper outline is like following a recipe. You need all of the key ingredients, and you need to know in what order they will be used. A properly developed claim will shape the rest of this "essay recipe" for you. Continue to add in the other "ingredients," or parts of the essay, to your outline "recipe." Use bullet points, snippets of quotations, and whatever notes you need to remind yourself of what you want to write. These are all of the important pieces of evidence that will help compose your essay. Be sure that each paragraph has a different group of ideas. No recipe asks you to repeat the same steps twice in a row, so make sure that you don't repeat your arguments. Sometimes two paragraphs will start to feel similar, or you may want to use the same examples in both paragraphs. In that case, consider merging the two paragraphs together to create one cohesive paragraph free of any repetition.

Sometimes it helps to visualize. Let's stick with the analogy of an outline as a recipe for your essay. What would that look like for this particular essay? Take a look below.

STEP 1 Introductory Paragraph

The ingredients you'll need for this step are a lead-in sentence, an overview of the topic, and a two-part claim, in that order. Be sure that your lead-in sentence draws in your reader. Make sure to provide a clear overview of the topic at hand. Finally, introduce a two-part claim that contains the topic and scope as well as your claim/stand/opinion.

STEP 2 Body Paragraph (Repeat for each body paragraph)

The ingredients you'll need for this step are a topic sentence, two to four pieces of evidence, a two-part commentary for each piece of evidence, a three-part counterargument, and a transition/conclusion sentence, in that order. The topic sentence discusses what the main focus of that paragraph will be. It should support the claim that you made in your introductory paragraph. The two to four pieces of evidence consist of quotations, data, facts, or personal examples that support your topic sentence. The two-part commentary for each piece of evidence provides a restatement of the evidence and then ties it back to the topic sentence and claim. For the three-part counterargument, you discuss what those on the other side of the issue say, why they are wrong, and how the fault in their argument ties back to the topic sentence of the paragraph. Finally, the transition/conclusion sentence briefly concludes that argument and transitions to the next paragraph. When deciding on the order of your body paragraphs, be sure to group similar ideas together, and make sure that everything is organized and flows clearly and logically.

STEP 3 Conclusion

The ingredients that you'll need for this step are a restatement of your original claim and a closing discussion, in that order. As discussed earlier in this chapter, restate your original claim, but try to reword it so as not to be repetitive. Finally, close out your discussion by returning to an overview of the overall topic. Be sure to briefly summarize all that was discussed in your essay, and leave the reader with a strong final statement that he or she will remember.

To see how this all would come together, let's return to the original claim to see how each part of the claim is used to create a paragraph.

Introduction	Body Paragraph One	Body Paragraph Two	Body Paragraph Three	Conclusion
Original Claim	Cause health issues	Create safety problems	Distract students from paying attention in class	Restated claim
Students should not be allowed to bring backpacks to class because they cause health issues, create safety problems, and distract students from paying attention in class.	Topic sentence: Students should not bring backpacks to class because they cause a number of health issues.	Topic sentence: When students bring backpacks to class, they create a safety hazard for teachers and classmates.	Topic sentence: Backpacks are full of items that students will use to distract themselves and their classmates from learning.	Since backpacks cause health issues, create safety problems, and distract students from paying attention in class, they should not be allowed in classrooms.

Do you have to write a five-paragraph essay? Sometimes yes, and in other cases no. Determining how you want to organize your ideas will determine the number of body paragraphs you will write. This outline necessitated a five-paragraph essay, but there are other options. You should aim to have an introductory paragraph, two to four body paragraphs, and a conclusion paragraph. **At the very least, you must have an introduction, one body paragraph, and a conclusion.**

 HELPFUL HINT

Don't try to fool the test graders by writing a lot! Only write what you need to. Don't try to fill up your essay with empty ideas just to take up more space. Writing more doesn't necessarily mean you will get a higher score—writing well does.

6. Write the Introduction

The **lead-in** should be a fast, short sentence that orients the reader to the subject. Sometimes it will be catchy or compelling, but a neutral sentence is just as good. Some students spend a lot of energy trying to create a dynamic "hook," which can sometimes be too far off topic. It isn't so much about being *clever* as it is about being *clear*.

The easiest way to include a good **overview** of the topic is to use the task as a guide. The test makers had to "introduce" the topic to you in the task, and you can "introduce" it right back to them in your introduction. However, be sure to use your own words. You are trying to give just enough information about the topic to get started. Do not include any real discussions here. If a stranger walked up to you on the street and hadn't seen any of the sources or the task, after reading your introductory paragraph, the stranger should have enough basic information on the topic to follow the rest of your essay.

The best location for your **claim** is following the overview of the topic. There is nothing more to introduce about the topic at that point. Going forward, you will need to elaborate on your claim, but you will do this in your body paragraphs. Take a look at the following sample introductory paragraph for this essay, and note the use of a lead-in, an overview, and a claim.

> **Sample Introduction: (Lead-in)** *Every day across this great nation, hundreds of students head off to school with backpacks filled with books, tablets, paper, and other supplies they need for the day.* **(Overview)** *While backpacks are a much-needed accessory for students, they can be harmful to the student's health. Regular use of backpacks can cause back problems, bad posture, and prolonged aches and pains. They also create other hazards in the classroom.* **(Claim)** *Students should not be allowed to bring backpacks to class because they cause health issues, create safety problems, and distract students from paying attention in class.*

7. Write the Body Paragraphs

The **topic sentence** announces what you will be discussing in each paragraph. It should also have some elements of your claim in it. This will help you maintain focus in the essay. Be sure to use **sign posts** (transition words) to introduce each point you are making within the paragraph. Announcing things in numerical order helps the reader track your ideas. For example,

> There are three ways of...
>
> The first way to...
>
> Another way to...
>
> The last way to...
>
> The author makes two points...
>
> The primary point...
>
> Secondly, the author states...

Be sure that each body paragraph tackles one part of your claim at a time and that you have two to four pieces of evidence per paragraph. Evidence can be a quotation from one of the sources, a fact from one of the sources, or even an example. Be sure to use quotation marks and cite the source when using exact quotations from source material. When paraphrasing source material, you do not have to use quotation marks, but you must cite the source used. For more details about the types of evidence that you could cite in your body paragraphs, refer back to Table 3-1 on page 46. For more information about how to introduce this evidence in your writing, refer back to Table 3-2 on page 47.

For the *argumentative essay* specifically, you will need to include a **three-part counterargument**. An easy way to do this is with the ***They say ... They are wrong because ... I say ...*** counterargument formula outlined in Table 4-3 on page 71. You can actually put a counterargument in many parts of the essay and still receive a strong score. Some students have enough information to create an entire counterargument body paragraph, but this isn't always possible. The safest way to be sure you are including the counterargument is to try to put one in each body paragraph that addresses the specific point the body paragraph is trying to make.

Table 4-3. Three-Part Counterargument Formula

Three-Part Counterargument	What do I write?	Example
a. They say…	Paraphrase or use a direct quotation that reflects the opposing point of view. Be sure to credit the source, if possible. Even if you don't have an exact quotation, you can still summarize an opposing argument.	In her article, "25 Terrible Things About Lockers," Shivani argues that students are often assigned lockers far from their friends' lockers.
b. They are wrong because…	In your own words, state the flaw in the opposing argument or why you disagree with that idea.	She neglects to explain how this is true for most students.
c. I say…	Tie it back to your claim.	Students should be focused on preparing for class by retrieving materials from their lockers. Students can visit with friends before and after school and at lunch. Carrying heavy backpacks in order to visit with friends is not worth the physical consequences.

The **transition/conclusion sentence** is the last part of the body paragraph, and it often mirrors the topic sentence. Reading the topic sentence and the transition/conclusion sentence side-by-side should make sense. If they don't read well side-by-side, you likely went off-track somewhere in the paragraph.

8. Write the Conclusion Paragraph

To write the conclusion, you should return to the background information you included in the introduction. Just give a fast **overview**. Do not introduce any new information in the conclusion. Tie up any loose ends. For instance, if you asked a question in the introduction, be sure to put the answer in the conclusion. You will need to **restate your claim** in a fresh way. Placing it near the end or at the end of the conclusion paragraph will create a feeling of finality. The conclusion will likely be the shortest paragraph in the essay. Take a look at the following sample conclusion paragraph for this essay.

Sample Conclusion: *Students may be annoyed at first by the new backpack ban, but they will ultimately be rewarded. Tripping hazards will be reduced. Crime on campus may decrease. Students will be able to stand taller and with less pain. Fewer toys and electronics will find their way into class. Students will be forced to organize their belongings more thoughtfully instead of constantly dumping more items into their backpacks. Since backpacks cause health issues, create safety problems, and distract students from paying attention in class, they should not be allowed in classrooms.*

9. Proofread

Review the task one last time to be sure that you did not leave out any parts of the required response in your essay. Leave enough time to proofread your essay. Sometimes students get tired during testing and want to finish as soon as possible so they rush through or skip proofreading altogether. However, leaving careless mistakes in your essay is like leaving money on the ground. If you can fix something, you should. An efficient method is to start at the end of the essay and read the last sentence, then the second to last sentence, then the third to last, moving backward, and so on. This method forces you to look at one sentence at a time to fix mistakes. Simply ask yourself, "Is this as clear as I can make it?" Finally, read it from the very beginning to the very end, making any final fixes.

10. Submit Your Essay

By this point, you've done all that you need to do, and you should be ready to submit your essay!

Narrative Strategies

This is creative writing. There are two types of narratives: **real** or **imagined**. The first part of the Performance Task will require you to examine multiple sources on a topic, take notes, and answer questions. The second part will either ask you to recall a real-life experience and write a story about what happened to you or it will ask you to write an imagined story. Unlike the argumentative and explanatory essays, for the narrative, you will *not* be expected to directly cite the sources. Instead, you should use them for inspiration and ideas. You can also make reference to them in your narrative if you think it is appropriate. You will need to plan your narrative, then write it and revise it if need be. When taking notes on the sources, you may want to start planning your story.

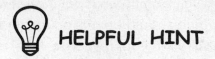 HELPFUL HINT

A **real narrative** is a true story. An **imagined narrative** is a story that you make up.

You will be scored on your ability to tell a complete story that stays on topic. You have to write a beginning, a middle, and an end, without detours. You must include elements of **plot**, **character**, and **setting**. If you remember your five Ws—*who, what, when, where,* and *why*—you will use them to cover most of this. You will also be asked to write from a certain **point of view**. Be sure to maintain that point of view throughout the narrative. The test graders expect that you will use many classic, story-telling **transition words** in your narrative. Be sure there is a clear ending to the story—there should not be any cliffhangers or loose ends. You don't need a conclusion paragraph, but you must make your story feel complete and finished.

The **development** and **elaboration** of your writing will also be evaluated. This includes many things. The first part, development, scores whether or not you told a complete story, while the next part, elaboration, scores how *developed* or *full* the story is. Including **details** in your writing is key. Graders will also be looking for **figurative language**. You should consider using *similes, metaphors, personification, hyperbole,* or other types of figurative language in your writing. Another great way to develop and elaborate your narrative is with **dialogue**. Finally, you will be scored on your **grammar**, **punctuation**, **capitalization**, and **spelling**. You are allowed to make a few mistakes, as long as they don't interfere with the meaning of the writing. Be sure to proofread your narrative before you submit it.

1. Orientation

Read the task and the directions. Ask yourself:

> * *What sort of story are they asking me to write?*
> * *Should the story be real or imagined?*
> * *What do the sources tell me?*

Think about the central ideas. The task will tell you exactly what point of view to write from. It will always indicate whether the writing should be real or imagined. Make sure you know exactly what details are required in your response. It is important that you **maintain your point of view** throughout the narrative—don't break character! What if the task asks you to write about something you have never experienced? You can always make up an experience; just make it believable. Table 4-4 provides some sample tasks along with the point of view required for that narrative and a determination of whether that task would require a real or imagined narrative.

Table 4-4. Point of View and Types of Narratives

Task	Point of View for the Narrative	Type of Narrative (Real or Imagined)
Imagine you are a new student at the school...	new student	imagined
Think back to a time when you were concerned about...	you	real
If you could design your dream amusement park...	you	imagined
Describe your favorite place to relax...	you	real
If you were an outdoor adventure leader, how would you...	outdoor adventure leader	imagined

Use your universal tools, such as the highlighter or the global notes, to help you. Quickly scan the sources, looking at the titles, any graphics, or any other interesting information. Once you have a sense of the task, you may begin examining the sources more closely.

To provide you with a clear example of how to follow the strategies for writing a narrative, throughout this section, we will refer to the "Enchanted Items Performance Task" on page 75.

ENCHANTED ITEMS PERFORMANCE TASK

Task:

An *enchanted* item is an object that has magical powers. These powers can be good or bad. You will read a Russian folktale and a mystery story in which there are enchanted items. You will answer some questions about the two sources. Then you will plan, write, and revise your own fictional narrative in which there is at least one enchanted item.

Directions:

To plan and compose your narrative, you will:

1. Read two stories, and take notes.

2. Answer questions about the sources.

3. Plan, write, and revise your narrative.

Clearly, this task is asking you to write a *fictional narrative*. The story must have *at least one enchanted item*. You will be provided with one Russian folktale and one mystery story as examples, so you can review those sources closely for ideas.

2. Examine the Sources

The test makers will supply multiple sources to provide you with many ideas for your narrative. These sources will give you an idea of exactly what sort of story you are supposed to be writing. Some tasks will ask you to be very imaginative, while others will ask for just a basic story. The sources provide the clues as to what the test graders are expecting. Use your universal tools to highlight information and gather ideas onto your global notes.

3. Respond to the Constructed-Response Tasks

The answers to these questions should be specific. Use exact language from the source, if possible, and give examples and details. Use the same strategies discussed in Chapter 3 regarding constructed-response tasks. Below is a sample constructed-response task for this Performance Task followed by a sample low-scoring student response and a sample high-scoring student response.

Constructed-Response Task: Explain how the enchanted items affect the main characters in the stories. Use details from the excerpts to support your answer.

Sample Low-Scoring Student Response

The enchanted items affect the characters in good and bad ways.

Sample High-Scoring Student Response

The enchanted items can be useful or hurtful to the characters. In "The Magic Coins," the servant's true, honest character is revealed by the coins when he sees a cure for his master's illness. In "The Strangest Jigsaw Ever," the magic puzzle ensures Lisa's demise as it lures her into its trap.

(Note that this response uses specific details and explanations to support the idea that the enchanted items can be helpful or hurtful.)

4. Create Your Plot Outline

Outline your **plot**. What will happen first? What will happen in the middle? What will happen at the end? Think of a way to start with action right away. You don't need an introductory paragraph (as you do for argumentative and explanatory essays). Steadily and logically, write a sequence of events that continuously builds upon each other. Be sure to put the moment with the greatest excitement or suspense—the climax—in the last paragraph. You won't need a conclusion paragraph in a narrative (as you do for argumentative and explanatory essays), but you will need one or two sentences that finish the story after the climax.

It is often helpful to visualize the plot outline to make sure that your narrative covers all necessary parts of the story. Below is a typical plot outline. Following this diagram is a sample narrative, broken down into the major parts of the story: the beginning, the middle, the climax, and the end.

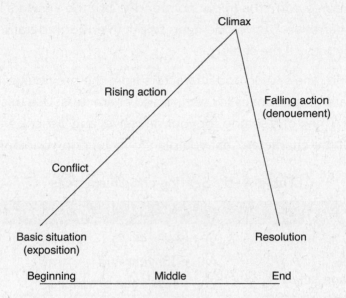

Beginning: Raul buys a bike at a garage sale.

Middle: Raul rides the bike, and it actually begins to fly! He finds that it is tricky to maneuver. Suddenly, he accidentally begins to travel into outer space. He struggles to get his bike to fly back home.

Climax: Raul panics when he realizes that he is stuck in space.

End: Raul figures out how to change direction on the bike, and he finally manages to fly his bike back home.

5. Jot Down Details About the Characters and the Setting

Consider who you need to include in your story (and who you can leave out). Start making some notes about each **character**. Think of personality traits, physical details, and what your characters want. What motivates them? What scares them? Do they have any unique qualities or quirks that can make them easy to picture? Don't forget to include their names. If you are the main character and the narrator, be sure to find ways to put details about yourself in the narrative, too. For example:

As a 13-year-old student, I never thought I would be in the position to...

My long brown hair often breaks free of my ponytail and whips me in the face while I am running the 50-meter dash...

Next, think about where the story will take place. Zoom in and out on the **setting** details. Where on a map does the story take place? What is the season? What is the year? What is the time of day? What is the weather like? What does the architecture look like? What color is the room? What is hanging on the walls? What is the mood (e.g., *tense*, *relaxed*, *joyful*)? You might not need to put the answers to all these questions in the narrative, but you do need to put in enough details so that the reader can clearly picture the setting.

Table 4-5 outlines the setting and characters from the previous example. Below these examples are empty boxes for setting and characters. Use this space to try this exercise yourself. Think of a setting for your narrative, and describe it in detail. Then write notes about the characters that you plan to include in your story.

Table 4-5. Setting and Characters

Setting	Characters

> Los Angeles
> Neighborhood
> Saturday garage sale
> Outside Earth's atmosphere
	> Raul
	  • 13-year-old
	  • Has four brothers
	  • Loves to fix up old bikes
	  • Short for his age, which bothers him
	> Bike (it's magical so it takes on characteristics of its own)
	  • Enchanted
	  • Can fly
	  • Hard to fly
	  • Used to belong to an inventor/wizard

6. Write the Narrative

Write the story. Be entertaining and add lots of details, but be sure to stick to the main story. Start with action, and get right into the story—for example, slam a door or start with some dialogue. Get the wheels rolling as quickly as possible. Below is a sample opener for this Performance Task.

Screech! Raul slammed on his bike's brakes. That was a close call! He nearly crashed into a broken piece of floating satellite. Accelerating the bike was extremely challenging outside of Earth's atmosphere. He couldn't believe he had traveled so far in just thirty minutes! It seemed like just a minute ago that he first laid eyes on the bike at the garage sale, and he just knew that he had to have it.

Whether the narrative is real or made up, you're creating a whole world, just like a film director. Movies are full of color, sound, action, and characters. If you were drawing, would your characters be like stick figures or like actual people? Is the setting blank or full of buildings? Are there moments of action and suspense? Include **details** in your writing, but don't write long-winded descriptions. You have to tell the story on the go—don't pause to give descriptions that are not central to the plot. Be sure to use **strong verbs**!

Let's take a look at some examples:

Description:

The children played at the park.

Better Description:

Paul screeched down the slide in his jeans, while Sarah hogged the swings, forcing Erik to find something else to do. Fortunately, Erik had dragged his enormous red plastic bucket and blue shovel to the park to sculpt the sand in the sandbox.

The second description is far better because it uses a lot of key details and verbs. Every child's action is announced separately and described in detail. From this example, you know exactly what every child was doing at the park. Furthermore, this example is full of strong verbs. A weaker example would say that Paul "went down" the slide. This example uses "screeched" to help the reader picture the sights and sounds in this story. Similarly, the writer could have said that Sarah "swung" on the swings. Instead, the phrase "hogged the swings" is used. This not only describes Sarah's actions, but it also shows a bit of her personality, that she is not letting anyone else go on the swings but her. Finally, Erik's description contains a couple of strong verbs. Rather than saying that he "brought" his bucket, the writer says that he "dragged" it, which helps the reader visualize that perhaps the bucket was too heavy for Erik to carry. Rather than saying that Erik wanted to "play with" the sand, the writer states that Erik planned to "sculpt" the sand, which makes the act seem like Erik is an artist molding clay.

Here's another example:

Description:

Summer camp was fun.

Better Description:

At Camp Piwanta, I worked with soft leather, making a wallet and a belt. I also cantered my horse, Chuckles, through the redwood cross-country course. One night, my cabin mate, Maria, and I scared one another with ghost stories. My first attempts at kayaking soaked me, but I would do it all again.

The second description is better because it includes more specific details about why camp was such a fun experience. The horse and the cabin mate are given names, which makes them more identifiable. Furthermore, each activity is described individually. There are also several strong verbs, such as "worked," "cantered," "scared," and "soaked."

With all of these descriptions, your goal should be to bring the story to life. If possible, try to provide descriptions for each of the **five senses**: touch, taste, sound, smell, and sight. Most writers tend to include visual details and sprinkle in a few sound details, but then leave out the other valuable details. Be sure to include as many details as you can.

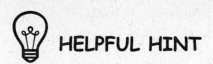 HELPFUL HINT

See if you can identify which sense is being used in each of the following descriptions:

I stroked the velvet pillow…

Chocolate chip cookies perfumed…

The roar of leaf-blowers woke…

My salty sweat dripped…

Millions of greens in the garden quilt shone…

(The answers are touch, smell, sound, taste, and sight.)

Include **transition words** to help guide the reader through your story. The list below is just a starter list; there are many more ways of doing this. Include a number of these words to help relate the sequence of events in your story.

Transition Words

above all	for this reason	likewise
after all	from	near
all of a sudden	further	not only... but
alongside	generally speaking	not to mention
although	given that	notably
another key point	here	obviously
as well as	however	of course
beyond	important to realize	regardless
by and large	in case	sooner or later
consequently	in effect	surprisingly
coupled with	in order to	then again
despite	in the beginning	there
especially	in the distance	to clarify
even though	in the first place	to say nothing of
eventually	in the hope that	whenever
finally	in the long run	with this in mind
for example	including	
for instance	instantly	

Also, don't forget to use **figurative language** in your writing. Your style of writing will determine what sort of figurative language to use. You might not be used to this, but attempt to use one or two of these types, if possible. Review Table 4-6 for some examples of figurative language.

Table 4-6. Figurative Language

Types	Definition	Example
Simile	A comparison of two things using *like* or *as*	*Her hair waved in the wind like a silk scarf.*
Metaphor	A direct comparison of two things (not using *like* or *as*)	*As she imagined the upcoming tournament, her face became a kaleidoscope of emotions.*
Personification	Language that gives a non-human subject human characteristics	*With its constant need for repair, the house swallowed most of its owners' money.*
Hyperbole	Extreme exaggeration	*I'd already failed a billion times, but today was going to be different.*

Be sure to also include some **dialogue**. You don't need a lot—a little goes a long way. Carefully format and punctuate it correctly. Be sure to start a new paragraph each time you switch speakers. Make clear use of dialogue tags (e.g., *he said*). The example below should remind you of how to use punctuation, capitalization, and indentation in dialogue.

"What?" he asked. "Are you crazy?"

"You never heard of 'taking a chance' before?" Carla started to walk toward the ride's line. She was going to conquer the roller coaster with or without him.

"Hey! Wait up! I want it try it just once," Stephen said, as he ran to catch up with her.

7. Revise

The word *revision* means "to see again," so read through your story with fresh eyes, looking for places where you can make the writing clearer or add an important detail. Ask yourself if you have answered **who**, **what**, **when**, **where**, and **why** in your story. In case you need a refresher, Table 4-7 outlines the key points to remember about who, what, when, where, and why when writing your narrative.

Table 4-7. Who, What, Where, When, and Why

Question	What You Need to Do	Descriptions to Include	How Much Detail Is Necessary
Who?	Create well-described characters	> Physical descriptions > Psychological descriptions (i.e., the characters' moods) > Fears/wants/needs > Names > Odd quirks, unique qualities > Relationships to other characters	A lengthy description isn't necessary. Slip a little description in as you go. Just be sure not to have talking heads without any characteristics.
What? (What happened?)	Create a complete plot	> Conflict(s) > Logical sequence of events > Climax	Get right to the point. Try to start with action, if you can. Don't include anything that isn't essential to the events of the story.
Where?	Create a complete setting	> Location > Weather > Up-close descriptions (i.e., rooms, things on the table, etc.)	Zoom in and out on the details.
When?	Create a complete setting	> Time > Year > Season	Zoom in and out on the details.
Why?	Explain why things are happening in the plot and why the characters are behaving the way they are	> Motivations > Expectations of events or people > Expected outcomes	Don't leave any questions for the reader.

When you're revising your narrative, ask yourself some key questions. Were you able to include descriptions that utilized the five senses? Does the story make sense? Are the characters fully developed, or are they only talking heads? Make sure that you continuously added details about the characters as the story unfolded. Did you include a brief amount of dialogue? Will the reader be able to imagine the setting? Did you continue to add setting descriptions throughout the narrative? Were you able to use a few examples of figurative language to enhance the story? If you answered yes to most of these questions, then your narrative should be in good shape!

8. Proofread

Leave enough time to proofread your narrative. Sometimes students get tired during testing and want to finish as soon as possible so they rush through or skip proofreading altogether. Just five to ten minutes of careful reading can enhance your final score. Remember, the most complete method is to start at the end of the story and read the last sentence, then the second to last, and so on. If any sentence is confusing, rewrite it until it is clear. After you have read through the story backwards, reread it from the very beginning to the very end, making any final edits.

9. Submit the Performance Task

By this point, you've done all that you need to do, and you should be ready to submit your narrative!

Practice Exercise

BACKPACKS PERFORMANCE TASK

Task:

Students may be in physical danger simply by carrying a heavy backpack, which can lead to serious health effects. However, many students believe backpacks help with organization. Some schools have responded by providing lockers for storage, but this might not be the answer either.

Should students be allowed to bring their backpacks to class? This is the subject of the article you will be writing for your school newspaper. In your research, you have come across three helpful sources arguing various angles of this debate.

In Part 1, you will carefully review these sources, and then you will answer some questions. Briefly scan the sources and the three questions that follow. In Part 2, you will write an argumentative essay on whether students should be allowed to bring their backpacks to class.

Directions:

1. Read all the sources, and take notes.

2. Answer three questions about the sources.

3. Plan and write your essay.

Part 1

Source Number 1—Backpack Safety: It's Time to Lighten the Load

(The following article was published by the National Safety Council, which is a nonprofit company that promotes health and safety in the United States.)

When you move your child's backpack after he or she drops it at the door, does it feel like it contains 40 pounds of rocks? Maybe you've noticed your child struggling to put it on, bending forward while carrying it, or complaining of tingling or numbness.

If you've been concerned about the effects that extra weight might have on your child's still-growing body, your instincts are correct.

Backpacks that are too heavy can cause a lot of problems for kids, like back and shoulder pain, and poor posture. The problem has grabbed the attention of lawmakers in some states, who have pushed for legislation requiring school districts to lighten the load.

While we wait for solutions like digital textbooks to become widespread, there are things you can do to help prevent injury. While it's common these days to see children carrying as much as a quarter of their body weight, the American Chiropractic Association recommends a full backpack weigh no more than 10 percent of a child's weight.

When selecting a backpack, look for:

- An ergonomic design

- The correct size: never wider or longer than your child's torso and never hanging more than 4 inches below the waist

- Padded back and shoulder straps

- Hip and chest belts to help transfer some of the weight to the hips and torso

- Multiple compartments to better distribute the weight

- Compression straps on the sides or bottom to stabilize the contents

- Reflective material

Remember: A roomy backpack may seem like a good idea, but the more space there is to fill, the more likely your child will fill it. Make sure your child uses both straps when carrying the backpack. Using one strap shifts the weight to one side and causes muscle pain and posture problems.

Help your child determine what is absolutely necessary to carry. If it's not essential, leave it at home.

What about backpacks on wheels?

They are so common these days, they're almost cool. But, the ACA is not giving them a strong endorsement.

Rolling backpacks should be used "cautiously and on a limited basis by only those students who are not physically able to carry a backpack," the ACA website reads. The reason? They clutter school corridors, replacing a potential back injury hazard with a tripping hazard.

So pick up that pack from time to time, and let your children know you've got their back.

Source Number 2—25 Terrible Things About Lockers (by Shivani)

Lockers are icons of the school experience. Typically, they're very useful for storing things … unfortunately, that's about it. I was never a locker fan for many reasons, mostly because I was lazy and disorganized, so walking extra distances to visit a paper vortex was not the top of my "fun things to do" list. But besides my laziness, there are lots of other things wrong with lockers:

1. They smell weird.

2. They're filled with random pits of food from past semesters.

3. You always get stuck with the locker next to the trash can.

4. Cleaning them out at the end of the year is a pain.

5. There's never enough space for your tennis racket.

6. You're always losing homework in the piles of loose-leaf paper and broken binders.

7. Opening the lock is basically impossible.

8. If you manage to get it open, you definitely can't close it.

9. What are those weird rust spots from?

10. The hooks break off and leave jagged locker shanks.

11. They only have one shelf, and it's not good for storage.

12. When people get theirs decorated for their birthday and you're a summer baby, you're left sad, jealous, and alone.

13. When the janitor is cleaning the hallway, you can't even get to your locker but you REALLY need to.

14. Not being able to visit your locker means you have to carry all your textbooks at the same time.

15. You have a 50% chance of getting the bottom locker.

16. If you're short, you'll always end up getting the top locker.

17. If you forget to visit your locker, you don't have any of your things for class.

18. Gym lockers.

19. Things like lacrosse sticks get stuck in lockers (they go in so easily and never come out).

20. Other people spray their lockers with perfume to counteract the weird smells, and you have to breathe the poisonous fumes.

21. You always get a locker on the opposite end of the school from your friends' lockers.

22. Trying to decorate the inside with cute photos and magnets usually ends in pathetic failure.

23. The vents are always dented, so no one can even slip notes into your locker.

24. If you need to visit your locker between classes, you're basically guaranteed to be in trouble for tardiness.

25. The paint chips off to reveal a weird '70s mustard shade.

Do you hate lockers?

Source Number 3—Which Backpacks Fit Into Lockers?

(The following blog and responses were posted on Eagle City Online Forum, which posts discussions about local city issues. The original post was made by "Mama.")

Eagle City Middle School has a new rule this fall that backpacks must stay in lockers during the day to avoid students hauling around their backpacks all day, straining their backs.

Locker measurements are: Height 34 inches, Depth 13 inches, Width 9 inches

Lands' End has a rolling backpack which is 18 inches by 12¾ inches by 8 inches which one would guess would fit and I have to order one soon. Anyone else have experience with this backpack?

Does anyone have ideas on which brands of backpacks will fit into lockers? His last rolling one did not fit but the wheels were so helpful.

Thanks, other parents.

Comments:

Posted by "Parent"

Students can take their books out of their backpack and organize their materials in their locker by order of classes that day. They can carry the books they need until they can get back to their locker. They will acquire organizational skills and be able to use any regular backpack that way.

Posted by "K"

I can't help on the specific backpack, we have always had to purchase very large and very well-built backpacks owing to a heavy book and materials load. We are long past being associated with this school, but I must say this is a great idea. I have been concerned for years with the extremely heavy backpacks many of our students must wear and anything to reduce that is a help. Certain texts in certain classes are quite heavy and must be carried almost every day to and from school and they are a burden at middle and especially at the high school level. I have seen students pulled over on their bikes from the weight of the backpacks (being off-balanced for a moment).

Posted by "Parent without handles"

The best backpacks are the ones the students will actually use.

The locker rule has been at our middle school for some time. It has to do with safety issues because there is no room in many classrooms for the two backpacks plus the musical instruments many students carry around school. All these backpacks take up too much space, and teachers complained that people were tripping over them and so the backpack in lockers rule came in. Musical instruments can usually be kept in music rooms when not in use. School backpacks and sports bags should be kept in lockers. Students leave them there before the first bell and carry what they need for their first two classes. Then at brunch and lunch, they exchange what they need for the next classes, lunch, etc.

This is all fine in theory. Many students now leave sweaters and so on in classrooms because there is nowhere for them to put them when they take them off, and they end up in the lost and found. Papers for one class are often left in other classes and other disorganization does happen. Textbooks should not be an issue because all heavy textbooks are duplicated so that there is one for home and one in the classroom so the only textbooks carried around should be slim music/math/language or paperback novels etc. If your child is carrying around heavy textbooks, talk to the teacher because they should not need to bring the one from home to school because there are more in the classroom.

Lastly, make sure your child likes the backpack you buy. You may think that the ones with wheels and organized pockets are great, but your child may be getting teased for having them. So make sure they get what they will use and not feel embarrassed about.

Posted by "Mama"

Also, now that my son and I think about it, the wheels do seem awkward… he was not embarrassed and did not get teased about it last year at school. I used to ask him why he didn't use his locker and he said that "everyone carries all their books around all day." I checked his backpack and realized that part of the reason it was heavy was due to the fact that it had wheels and a handle!

Posted by "It's a good thing…"

Backpacks staying in lockers is a good thing. Not only does it prevent theft from the classroom, but it also provides for a safer campus as well.

Posted by "K"

Actually, there have been several locker break-ins and students' stuff has been strewn all about.

Posted by "lockers…"

Lockers are completely safe. 99% of the time during locker theft, the owner of the locker did one of three things:

1) He didn't lock his locker for some reason.

2) He left his lock ready to be opened with a simple pull. In this scenario, students close their locker, put their lock on it, and then begin to open the lock again, stopping on the last number. All someone has to do is pull down on the lock and it opens.

3) He told one of his "friends" his locker combination.

Don't do any of these things and you're fine.

Constructed-Response Tasks

Now that you've read all three sources, use your remaining time to complete the three tasks that follow. Your responses to these tasks will be scored. Also, they will help you think about the sources you've read, which should help you write your essay. You may refer back to the sources when you think it would be helpful. You may also refer to your notes. Complete the tasks in the spaces provided.

1. Explain the health issues students face as a result of using backpacks. Use details from the sources to support your answer. Write your answer in the box below.

2. Explain why students might hesitate to use lockers. Use details from the sources to support your answer. Write your answer in the box below.

3. What are the benefits of students wearing backpacks to class? Use details from the sources to support your answer. Write your answer in the box below.

(Answers are on page 158.)

Part 2

Now review your notes and sources, and then plan, draft, and revise your essay. You may use your notes and refer back to the sources. You may also refer to your responses to the constructed-response tasks at the end of Part 1, but you cannot change those answers. Now read your assignment and the information about how your essay will be scored, and then begin your work.

Your Assignment:

Your class is writing articles for the school newspaper on whether or not students should be allowed to bring backpacks to class. Write an argumentative essay that answers the following questions:

> What are the health and safety concerns for students wearing backpacks?
> What are the different ways in which students can avoid injury from wearing a backpack?
> Are lockers a solution to the health concerns?

Support the statements you make in your essay with details from the sources you read.

Argumentative Essay Scoring:

Your argumentative essay will be scored using the following:

1. **Organization/Purpose:** How well did you state your claim, address opposing claims, and maintain your claim with a logical progression of ideas from beginning to end? How well did you use transitions to explain your ideas? How effective were your introduction and your conclusion?

2. **Evidence/Elaboration:** How well did you use relevant and specific information from the sources? How well did you elaborate on your ideas? How well did you clearly state ideas in your own words? How well did you cite references to the sources you used?

3. **Conventions:** How well did you follow the rules for punctuation, capitalization, and spelling?

Now begin work on your essay. Manage your time carefully so that you have time to:

> Plan your essay
> Write your essay
> Revise and edit for a final draft

Use the work space below, and additional scratch paper if needed, to write your essay. (Note that sample responses to this essay can be found beginning on page 161.)

Practice Test

During the testing window, you will take both parts of the SBAC Grade 8 ELA exam on a computer. When working through this practice test, try to recreate the testing environment as best as you can. Set aside the recommended amount of time for each part of the test, and be sure your testing environment is as free of distractions as possible. Have scratch paper, a pencil, and a highlighter nearby. For the Performance Task, have a hard copy of a dictionary and a thesaurus available. You will need to practice using these offline, so do not use a dictionary or a thesaurus on the computer. Take either the CAT or the Performance Task by itself, but do not try to take more than one of these in one sitting. All of the answers and explanations to the questions on both parts of this practice test can be found in Chapter 6.

Computer Adaptive Test

Directions: The actual CAT will be computer adaptive, meaning that the questions will become easier, harder, or stay the same depending on whether you answer the questions correctly or incorrectly. Since you are taking this test in a book, the test will not adjust based on your answers. Therefore, you need to review every question carefully, and be aware of how much time you have left. You should allot yourself approximately 1 hour and 30 minutes to take the CAT. Remember that you can take breaks.

Section 1

(You must respond to all the tasks in this section before you can move on to the next section.)

Directions: Maps are helpful for looking up a location; however, they had multiple purposes in early America. Read the following informational article, "Maps," and respond to tasks 1-5.

Maps

Studying old maps of the American colonies and the United States reveals the story of how Europeans took possession of the land. As soon as the first ships came to America, the first order of action was claiming the land and its bounty. Once the land was claimed, the very next task was documenting where the land was, through a written description of the area and through drawing a map. The claims and maps were sent to government officials and to the investors who wanted to see what their investment had obtained. The success of the colonies, and later on the United States, was dependent on the acquisition of land. As a result, acre-by-acre maps were drawn of the sprawling growth.

Affluent people often displayed these maps prominently as symbols of wealth and status. Some maps were commissioned to be displayed in specific parts of the home. Frequently, maps were displayed in hallways or on stairways—the most visible spaces in the home. Another popular place to display a map was in the dining room, where guests would eat and converse. The owners of the maps would hope that such displays would show their worldly and scientific interests. Not only would the owner of such maps be considered wealthy, but he would also be considered intelligent by everyone who visited.

Maps were also used as propaganda. Building infrastructure, like bridges, roads, and canals, is expensive. Obtaining money for these projects is always difficult, but maps helped visually show the need for the infrastructure by showing the geographical challenges posed by the land. Maps also created a concrete image for a solution to transportation problems. It is only as a result of maps that many projects were approved.

Ship captains needed to know the safest routes through tricky waters. Suppliers wanted to know the fastest and safest passages by which to travel. Very little of the continent had been charted, and the need for dependable maps was essential for the development of businesses. Most businesses relied on trade, and reliable trade routes helped with their success. As the colonies expanded westward, they traded mostly on water routes, which were much less expensive and faster than trying to travel by land. Journeys by land were often bumpy and would damage goods.

Reliable maps were important in every military effort in North America. During the French and Indian War, the British and the French were in deep dispute over the land, which had not been well documented. Whichever side had the more accurate map had the military advantage in fighting. A thorough geographical map was essential in the Revolutionary and Civil Wars, too. George Washington very famously crossed the Delaware River in the middle of the night and was able to shift the outcome of the Revolutionary War. You better believe General Washington consulted a map in order to make such an important journey.

1. In the sentence, "Affluent people often displayed these maps prominently as symbols of wealth and status," what does the word "affluent" mean?

    O   A.   wealthy
    O   B.   influential
    O   C.   fluent
    O   D.   important

2. What is the author's main message in this article?

    O   A.   Wealthy people like maps.
    O   B.   Maps had many purposes for early Americans.
    O   C.   The Revolutionary War was won because of a map.
    O   D.   Maps were essential for trade and business.

3. Reread the fourth paragraph, which is reprinted below:

"Ship captains needed to know the safest routes through tricky waters. Suppliers wanted to know the fastest and safest passages by which to travel. Very little of the continent had been charted, and the need for dependable maps was essential for the development of businesses. Most businesses relied on trade, and reliable trade routes helped with their success. As the colonies expanded westward, they traded mostly on water routes, which were much less expensive and faster than trying to travel by land. Journeys by land were often bumpy and would damage goods."

Which sentence from this paragraph could be moved to the beginning of this paragraph as the new topic sentence to create a more logical sequence of ideas? Write your answer in the box below.

4. Which of the following options would be a stronger title for the article than "Maps"?

O A. "How to Have a Dinner Party with a Map"
O B. "A Brief History of Maps in Early America"
O C. "Without a Map, the Early Colonial Shipping Businesses Would Have Sunk"
O D. "Mapping Early America"

5. Reread this sentence from the second paragraph.

"Not only would the owner of such maps be considered wealthy, but he would also be considered intelligent by everyone who visited."

Using information from the article, explain why hanging a map in the dining room would make a person seem intelligent. Write your answer in the box below.

Section 2

(You must respond to all the tasks in this section before you can move on to the next section.)

Directions: A student is writing an explanatory essay on Chinese New Year traditions. Read the outline below, and respond to tasks 1–3.

The Chinese New Year Explanatory Essay Outline

I. Introduction of the Chinese New Year celebrations

    A. Begins a new lunar calendar

II. Preparing for the Chinese New Year

    A. Houses cleaned

    B. Windows washed

    C. Coincides with the start of spring

    D. Curtains cleaned

    E. Brooms and brushes hidden

    F. All debts paid or reduced

    G. Parade floats

    H. Offerings made in the temple to honor ancestors

    I. New clothes bought

    J. Hair is not washed, so as not to "wash away" good luck

    K. Banquets and reunions attended

    L. At midnight, doors and windows opened to let the "old year" out

III. Home decorations

    A. Branches of peaches, almonds, or apricots

    B. Pears are avoided because "separation" and "pear" are the same word in Chinese

    C. Calligraphy of "good luck" is hung

    D. Red lanterns

E. Images of the Chinese zodiac are hung

F. Traditional foods, including narcissus and daffodil bulbs, are prepared

G. Fruit arrangement: oranges, kumquats, and tangerines

    1. The sweetness symbolizes a "sweet life"

IV. Chinese New Year parade

A. Firecrackers

    1. Supposed to scare away bad spirits

B. Cymbals, drums, and metal gongs

C. *Lai see*: lucky red money envelopes given to friends and family

    1. The amount of money should be in even numbers (odd numbers are associated with funerals)

D. Coincides with the start of spring

E. Lion dancers

    1. Papier-mâché head

    2. Head painted red, yellow, green, and orange

F. Dragon

    1. Breathes real fire and smoke

    2. Zig-zags down the street

    3. Brings rainfall

    4. Symbolizes the Emperor

    5. Appears at the Chinese New Year

    6. Importance of the Chinese New Year celebration

1. Rearrange "The Chinese New Year Explanatory Essay Outline" to better organize the ideas in the essay. Write your answer in the box below.

2. Using the "The Chinese New Year Explanatory Essay Outline," which of the following sentences might be found in the "Chinese New Year parade" paragraph? Place a check mark next to all that apply.

   ☐ People clean their houses thoroughly, even washing the windows in preparation.

   ☐ Lion heads are created out of papier-mâché and painted red, yellow, green, and orange.

   ☐ The dragon, which symbolizes the Emperor, zig-zags down the street, breathing real fire and smoke.

   ☐ Families visit temples to make offerings to their ancestors because this shows respect for the dead; the ancestors are asked to protect their descendants.

3. Using the "The Chinese New Year Explanatory Essay Outline," write the paragraph for the section of the outline that is labeled "Home decorations." Be sure to include all parts of that paragraph as discussed in the outline. Use the box below to write your answer.

Section 3

(You must respond to all the tasks in this section before you can move on to the next section.)

Directions: Read the poem below, in which Walt Whitman writes about the death of President Abraham Lincoln, and respond to tasks 1–4.

O Captain! My Captain!

by Walt Whitman

O Captain! my Captain! our fearful trip is done,

The ship has weather'd every rack, the prize we sought is won,

The port is near, the bells I hear, the people all exulting,

While follow eyes the steady keel, the vessel grim and daring;

But O heart! heart! heart!

O bleeding drops of red,

Where on the deck my Captain lies,

Fallen cold and dead.

O Captain! my Captain! rise up and hear the bells;

Rise up—for you the flag is flung—for you the bugle trills,

For you bouquets and ribbon'd wreaths—for you the shores a-crowding,

For you they call, the swaying mass, their eager faces turning;

Here Captain! dear father!

This arm beneath your head!

It is some dream that on the deck,

You've fallen cold and dead.

My Captain does not answer, his lips are pale and still,

My father does not feel my arm, he has no pulse or will,

This ship is anchor'd safe and sound, its voyage closed and done,

From fearful trip the victor ship comes in with object won;

Exult O shores, and ring O bells!

But I with mournful tread,

Walk the deck my Captain lies,

Fallen cold and dead.

1. Choose all of the following that are true for the poem "O Captain! My Captain!"

☐ A. *Captain* and *the ship* are both part of a metaphor for the United States of America during Civil War times.

☐ B. "People all exulting" refers to people excited to end the Civil War.

☐ C. "Where on the deck my Captain lies" shows that the Captain has slipped and fallen on the deck.

☐ D. The "Captain," the "father," and "you" are all President Abraham Lincoln.

2. Which of the following is an example of *irony* in the poem?

O A. The Captain does not answer because he has died.

O B. The Captain dies just as the ship arrives at the port.

O C. The journey was a difficult one.

O D. Someone has dreamed about the deck.

3. Which of the following would be reasons why Whitman repeated the phrase, "fallen cold and dead"? Select all that apply.

☐ A. Whitman wanted the reader to think of the *fall* of President Lincoln and the aftermath of his assassination.

☐ B. Whitman wanted to show the reader how bad the weather was.

☐ C. Whitman wanted to emphasize the shock and severity of President Lincoln's death.

☐ D. Whitman didn't know how to write about death in any other way.

4. Explain why Whitman addresses President Lincoln as "my Captain" in this poem. Write your answer in the box below.

Section 4

(You must respond to all the tasks in this section before you can move on to the next section.)

Directions: The westward expansion of the United States created challenges for the land that had existed for thousands of years and also for the new settlers. Read the article "The Dust Bowl and Dust Storms of the 1930s," and respond to tasks 1–7.

The Dust Bowl and Dust Storms of the 1930s

Before European-Americans moved westward to settle, the Great Plains region of the United States was rich and robust. For thousands of years, this huge expanse of land was covered with hardy prairie grasses that would grow as much as six feet high above the soil and nine feet below the soil. Nourishing soil was held to the earth by these wet, plentiful grasses. Prairie grass is at the root of the Great Plains ecosystem. It sustained wild herds, including millions of buffalo, which, in turn, provided food for prey. Even Native Americans lived as part of this balanced ecosystem. Harsh, snowy winters and scorching summers only strengthened the grasses. Not even drought could wipe them out. Even after being trodden by the herds, the grasses remained almost indestructible. That is, until the arrival of the eastern settlers.

In 1803, the U.S. government bought a lot of land, west of the Mississippi River, from France as part of the Louisiana Purchase. Lewis and Clark were sent to explore the newly acquired land in 1804. They returned in 1806 and presented reports of the exploration to the U.S. Congress. These reports included vivid descriptions of the Great Plains, which sounded like promising farm land. The U.S. Government and its people became eager to populate and settle throughout the plains area. Free or inexpensive land lured the people westward, and, by the late 1800s, much of the open prairie was filling up with thousands of settlers.

In order to farm, millions of acres of prairie grasses were pulled. The land was plowed and seeded with new crops. The invention of the tractor and the need for wheat in World War I tempted farmers to plant as much as they could. The farmers were happy with the results, but they couldn't have known that 1910 to 1930 were particularly rainy years, which helped their crops flourish. The area grew quickly, as little towns popped up everywhere. Since they had only recently emigrated, the farmers couldn't have known how unusual the weather had been during these years.

The 1930s were more difficult years for the United States in general, but especially so for the farmers on the plains. The horrible stock market crash of 1929, followed by the Great Depression left banks without money and millions of people without jobs. It also forced the price of wheat to drop significantly. The farmers were not able to make money on the wheat crops, and, to make things worse, the drought that started in 1932 actually caused an exorbitant number of crops to wither and die. All the wonderful rain during the previous two decades had set up the false premise that these pastures were constantly watered but in fact this area was actually quite arid. The prairie grasses that had held the topsoil to the earth were gone and so was the topsoil. The vacant fields dried up and started to blow away, which made a bad problem worse.

The Southern Plains, including portions of Colorado, Kansas, New Mexico, eastern Oklahoma, and the panhandle of Texas, were especially susceptible to the drought. This area eventually became known as the Dust Bowl because all the fields that were blowing away were creating natural disasters. Dust storms frequently occurred in this area and forced families off their farms to look for jobs in the west, like California. Millions of acres of wheat were destroyed by these storms. Even though these families came from several different states, all were called "okies." By the middle of the 1930s, thousands of families had lost everything and had given up hope for this area, taking their meager possessions and families westward.

Dust storms are an amazing phenomenon to witness. A dust storm can gather in a matter of seconds, rise up and expand to block out the sun, and swallow whole towns and farms. It needs only two elements to occur: some loose, dry dust and a breeze or wind over nine miles an hour. The way the dust particles blow around and strike each other actually makes the dust storm grow bigger once it has started. Some storms grow so large that they start to create their own weather phenomenon. Thunder, lightning, fierce winds, and even precipitation can occur. If the conditions are just right, a dust storm can rise up and overtake an entire city in a matter of minutes.

Think of how annoying it is to get sand in your eyes. Now imagine all the air swirling with dirt hitting you and blackening the sky. There is fine dust as well as gritty dust, and it gets everywhere. The heavier dust grates and scratches like sandpaper, causing damage to the skin and other objects. The fine dust sneaks in through closed doors and windows and kills machinery and humans. Many people breathed in the dangerous dust and needed to go to hospitals to be treated for "dust pneumonia."

During these years, people tried to adapt by covering plates and food with cloths until dinner time or by wearing kerchiefs and goggles over their faces when outside. Dust storms further destroyed meager crops. Millions of acres of wheat fields were destroyed. Even during the scorching summers, people would keep their doors and windows closed in hopes of keeping the dust out. During a dust storm, the conditions eerily block out most sound, cutting off all sounds and sights. The psychological effects of living in the dusty and hard economic conditions were too much to take.

As these conditions continued, people began to understand the mistake of removing the prairie grasses. Life was becoming more desperate for those who chose to remain and even for those further east. On May 11, 1934, a huge dust storm gathered force, collecting millions of tons of topsoil and transporting it well over a thousand miles to the eastern seaboard of the United States. People in New York, Boston, and Atlanta, and even on boats 300 miles out to sea, were choking on dust. This was helpful, however, as there were some in Congress who were trying to get something done about restoring and preserving the soil conditions of the Dust Bowl area for the future. One congressman simply pointed to the dusty conditions outside the windows to make his point.

The worst dust storm occurred on Sunday, April 14, 1935. For weeks people had been suffering from the dusty conditions, but on that Sunday people woke up to clear, blue skies and fresh air. Then a slight breeze started and gathered momentum. By the afternoon, the largest dust storm on record in the United States was barreling across the nation. It grew to epic proportions of 200 miles wide (as wide as Indiana) and 8,000 feet high (as high as a substantial mountain). There was enough dust to fill up basements and to bury towns. The dust scratched thousands of people, like tiny razors. Visibility was reduced significantly. Cars ran off roads because their lights were useless in the storm. People wandered for hours in the storm looking for home; in some instances, they were only 100 feet from their houses, but couldn't see them. Lightning and thunder punctuated the constant barrage of dust. Most people huddled together for hours waiting for the storm to blow away. This horrible day became known as "Black Sunday."

The storm was so bad that many felt it was time to change farming practices. A short while later, as part of the "New Deal," President Franklin D. Roosevelt enforced farming regulations like crop rotation, seeding, and new plowing techniques. The new regulations were called Soil Conservation Service (SCS) in the Department of Agriculture. Not only did the SCS create farming regulations, but it also gave financial assistance to farmers who adopted Roosevelt's ideas. This federal aid made a huge difference in the lives of the farmers and also the farms themselves. These new practices reduced the dust by 65 percent. Prairie grasses were planted once again, and the strength of the grasses began to heal the area. In 1939, the rains returned, although periods of drought are always going to be part of that region. As a result of more thoughtful conservation of the soil, the U.S. hasn't had a catastrophic dust storm since, although many other parts of the world have to live with regular dust storms.

1. Reread the following sentence from the third paragraph of this article.

"The invention of the tractor and the need for wheat in World War I tempted farmers to plant as much as they could."

What can you infer about farming during this time period based on this sentence?

O A. Farmers were worried about having enough to eat during World War I, so they planted more wheat.
O B. The tractor reduced the amount of labor used, so farmers had more time to expand their wheat planting.
O C. The demand for wheat was high during World War I. The invention of the tractor saved farmers time so they were able to plant more wheat, allowing them to make more money.
O D. Soldiers used tractors and wheat to harvest during World War I.

2. "Prairie grass is at the root of the Great Plains ecosystem" is an example of what form of figurative language?

O A. metaphor
O B. hyperbole
O C. pun
O D. alliteration

3. Reread the following sentence from the fourth paragraph.

"The farmers were not able to make money on the wheat crops, and, to make things worse, the drought that started in 1932 actually caused an exorbitant number of crops to wither and die."

What does the word "exorbitant" mean in this context?

O   A.   highly excessive
O   B.   unnecessary
O   C.   nearby
O   D.   healthy

4. Reread the topic sentence from the sixth paragraph.

"Dust storms are an amazing phenomenon to witness."

Which quote from the article best supports this topic sentence?

O   A.   "If the conditions are just right, a dust storm can rise up and overtake an entire city in a matter of minutes."
O   B.   "Millions of acres of wheat were destroyed by these storms."
O   C.   "These new practices reduced the dust by 65 percent."
O   D.   "Life was becoming more desperate for those who chose to remain and even for those further east."

5. In paragraph four, reprinted below, circle the two words that should be followed by a comma.

"The 1930s were more difficult years for the United States in general, but especially so for the farmers on the plains. The horrible stock market crash of 1929, followed by the Great Depression left banks without money and millions of people without jobs. It also forced the price of wheat to drop significantly. The farmers were not able to make money on the wheat crops, and, to make things worse, the drought that started in 1932 actually caused an exorbitant number of crops to wither and die. All the wonderful rain during the previous two decades had set up the false premise that these pastures were constantly watered but in fact this area was actually quite arid. The prairie grasses that had held the topsoil to the earth were gone and so was the topsoil. The vacant fields dried up and started to blow away, which made a bad problem worse."

6. Reread the following excerpt from paragraph seven, and edit it so that it maintains a formal style and an objective tone. Write your answer in the box below.

"Think of how annoying it is to get sand in your eyes. Now imagine all the air swirling with dirt hitting you and blackening the sky. There is fine dust as well as gritty dust, and it gets everywhere."

7. Reread the following sentences from the ninth paragraph.

"People in New York, Boston, and Atlanta, and even on boats 300 miles out to sea, were choking on dust. This was helpful, however, as there were some in Congress who were trying to get something done about restoring and preserving the soil conditions of the Dust Bowl area for the future. One congressman simply pointed to the dusty conditions outside the windows to make his point."

Create an argument that the congressman might possibly have made on that day. Write your answer in the box below.

Section 5

(You must respond to all the tasks in this section before you can move on to the next section.)

Directions: Read the following essay, and respond to tasks 1–8.

Not Everyone Celebrates Birthdays the Same Way

Throughout history, birthday traditions have changed considerably, and from one culture to another, celebrations vary greatly. It is believed that the first birthday celebrations started in ancient Egypt. When royals were crowned, it was believed that they became gods. The coronation was a type of birth, and the day of coronation was celebrated with elaborate feasts. As far as we know, the Romans were the first culture to celebrate the birthday of someone who was not royalty.

The American tradition of the birthday party also has a varied history, with origins in Germany. For the last 200 years, Germans have celebrated birthdays by setting out cakes in the morning and lighting candles held in a special candelabra. At the end of the day, the candles are blown out, and the cake is eaten. By the mid-19th century, sugar beets were more widely cultivated, allowing for the production of sugar from Europe. This made sugar less expensive to produce locally, as Europeans no longer had to wait for costly shipping from warmer locations where cane sugar grows. Since sugar was more affordable, more Americans and Europeans were able to make cakes, allowing for the annual production of birthday cakes.

Around 1900, party decorations and favors became a more familiar sight at birthday celebrations, and the modern idea of a children's party was firmly established in the 1950s, involving guests, games, cake, candles, and presents. By this time, making a wish and blowing out candles became a tradition. Some people even make a wish when slicing the birthday cake. It is considered bad luck to take a bite of cake before the birthday boy or girl takes a bite. "Happy Birthday to You" is a very traditional singing experience for most people, although it hasn't been around that long. Most people believe that tune was based on the melody of "Good Morning to All," written by Patty and Mildred J. Hill in 1893. By most accounts, "Happy Birthday to You" is the most famous song in the world. Ever since that song was written, it has been riddled with copyright controversies.

As with other celebrations, many cultures share traditions through the various channels of cultural exchange. Germany has another birthday tradition that has been adopted by several cultures. Sometimes friends will sneak up on the birthday boy or girl and throw flour in his or her face, sometimes called "antiquing" a person. This is very popular in Jamaica, too. Hungary's traditional practice of tugging on the birthday boy's or girl's ear can be found on the other side of the world in Argentina, where the earlobe is tugged once for each year the person has been alive. The "spanking machine," where the birthday boy or girl crawls through a lineup of friends and relatives to be playfully spanked, is similar to the United Kingdom's tradition of turning the birthday boy or girl upside down and "bumping" him or her on the ground once for each year he or she has been alive, plus an additional bump for luck. Scotland seems to be the origin of a popular Canadian birthday tradition about luck. "Nose grease," or butter, is put on the birthday boy's or girl's nose so bad luck will slip off. In Brazil, they crack an egg on the head of the birthday person, also for luck. A red envelope filled with money and good luck is given in both Malaysia and Vietnam. However, in Vietnam, a person's birthday is celebrated on the Lunar New Year, not on the anniversary of a person's birth. This means that everyone celebrate their birthdays on the same day. The Chinese eat *shou mian* or "long-life noodles" on one's birthday. The birthday person symbolically slurps in as much of the long noodle as possible before biting to wish for a long life. Somalians do not celebrate birthdays at all and instead celebrate the death day of loved ones. "Fairy bread," which is white buttered bread covered with sprinkles, is a popular birthday treat in New Zealand and Australia and is served in lieu of birthday cake. Mexicans festively hang piñatas filled with candy and then, while blindfolded, beat the piñata open with a broomstick. One culture's idea of birthday fun seems to inspire the next culture's traditions.

As we get to know more about people around the world, we are likely to adopt new celebrations from other cultures. What new tradition will you adopt this year?

1. This question has two parts. First, answer Part A. Then answer Part B.

Part A

Which of the following statements summarizes the central idea of the essay?

- ○ A. "Germany has another birthday tradition that has been adopted by several cultures."
- ○ B. "As we get to know more about people around the world, we are likely to adopt new celebrations from other cultures."
- ○ C. "As far as we know, the Romans were the first culture to celebrate the birthday of someone who was not royalty."
- ○ D. "Since sugar was more affordable, more Americans and Europeans were able to make cakes, allowing for the annual production of birthday cakes."

Part B

From the choices below, select the details from the essay that best support your answer to Part A. Select all that apply.

- ☐ A. "The American tradition of the birthday party also has a varied history, with origins in Germany."
- ☐ B. "By the mid-19th century, sugar beets were more widely cultivated, allowing for the production of sugar from Europe."
- ☐ C. "Most people believe that tune was based on the melody of 'Good Morning to All,' written by Patty and Mildred J. Hill in 1893."
- ☐ D. "Hungary's traditional practice of tugging on the birthday boy's or girl's ear can be found on the other side of the world in Argentina, where the earlobe is tugged once for each year the person has been alive."

2. Reread the following sentence from the fourth paragraph.

"'Fairy bread,' which is white buttered bread covered with sprinkles, is a popular birthday treat in New Zealand and Australia and is served in lieu of birthday cake."

In this context, what does "in lieu" mean?

- ○ A. on top
- ○ B. instead
- ○ C. alongside
- ○ D. with

3. Reread the following sentence from the first paragraph.

"As far as we know, the Romans were the first culture to celebrate the birthday of someone who was not royalty."

Which of the following statements can we infer from this sentence? Select all that apply.

☐ A. We don't have a lot of information about the history of non-royal birthdays before Roman history.

☐ B. Romans really liked to party.

☐ C. Everyone in Roman society was highly respected.

☐ D. Other cultures may have celebrated non-royal birthdays, but we have not discovered enough evidence yet to make that claim.

4. Reread the following sentences from the fourth paragraph.

"The Chinese eat *shou mian* or 'long-life noodles' on one's birthday. The birthday person symbolically slurps in as much of the long noodle as possible before biting to wish for a long life."

Based on these sentences, what can you infer that "symbolically slurping" the noodles means?

O A. Slurping noodles is lucky.

O B. To make a wish, the birthday person must slurp noodles.

O C. The longer the noodle slurped, the longer the life of the birthday person.

O D. Eating *shou mian* is essential to living a long life.

5. In this essay, how many sentences contain references to wishes or luck?

O A. 5

O B. 7

O C. 9

O D. 11

6. Reread the following sentences from the fourth paragraph.

"However, in Vietnam, a person's birthday is celebrated on the Lunar New Year, not on the anniversary of a person's birth. This means that everyone *celebrate* their birthdays on the same day."

From the following list of replacements, select the best word or phrase to replace the italicized word in this excerpt.

> celebrates
>
> celebration
>
> have celebrated
>
> celebrating

7. Reread the following sentences from this essay.

"One culture's idea of birthday fun seems to inspire the next culture's traditions.

As we get to know more about people around the world, we are likely to adopt new celebrations from other cultures. What new tradition will you adopt this year?"

Which of the following statements most likely describes why the author ends the essay with these three sentences?

- O A. The author wants the reader to throw a birthday party for many different cultures.
- O B. The author wants to inform the reader about birthday traditions from around the world.
- O C. The author hopes the reader will be open-minded about trying out other types of birthday celebrations honored in other cultures.
- O D. The author wants the reader to travel more in the future.

8. In a multi-paragraph response, describe your own birthday traditions. Write your answer in the box below.

Section 6

(You must respond to all the tasks in this section before you can move on to the next section.)

Directions: Read the autobiographical story, "The Beadwork," from *American Indian Stories* in which Zitkala-Sa, a Dakota Sioux Indian, discusses a memory from her childhood, and then respond to tasks 1–3.

The Beadwork

by Zitkala-Sa

Soon after breakfast mother sometimes began her beadwork. On a bright, clear day, she pulled out the wooden pegs that pinned the skirt of our wigwam to the ground, and rolled the canvas part way up on its frame of slender poles. Then the cool morning breezes swept freely through our dwelling, now and then wafting the perfume of sweet grasses from newly burnt prairie.

Untying the long tasseled strings that bound a small brown buckskin bag, my mother spread upon a mat beside her bunches of colored beads, just as an artist arranges the paints upon his palette. On a lapboard she smoothed out a double sheet of soft white buckskin; and drawing from a beaded case that hung on the left of her wide belt a long, narrow blade, she trimmed the buckskin into shape. Often she worked upon small moccasins for her small daughter. Then I became intensely interested in her designing. With a proud, beaming face, I watched her work. In imagination, I saw myself walking in a new pair of snugly fitting moccasins. I felt the envious eyes of my playmates upon the pretty red beads decorating my feet.

Close beside my mother I sat on a rug, with a scrap of buckskin in one hand and an awl in the other. This was the beginning of my practical observation lessons in the art of beadwork. From a skein of finely twisted threads of silvery sinews my mother pulled out a single one. With an awl she pierced the buckskin, and skillfully threaded it with the white sinew. Picking up the tiny beads one by one, she strung them with the point of her thread, always twisting it carefully after every stitch.

It took many trials before I learned how to knot my sinew thread on the point of my finger, as I saw her do. Then the next difficulty was in keeping my thread stiffly twisted, so that I could easily string my beads upon it. My mother required of me original designs for my lessons in beading. At first I frequently ensnared many a sunny hour into working a long design. Soon I learned from self-inflicted punishment to refrain from drawing complex patterns, for I had to finish whatever I began.

After some experience I usually drew easy and simple crosses and squares. These were some of the set forms. My original designs were not always symmetrical nor sufficiently characteristic, two faults with which my mother had little patience. The quietness of her oversight made me feel strongly responsible and dependent upon my own judgment. She treated me as a dignified little individual as long as I was on my good behavior; and how humiliated I was when some boldness of mine drew forth a rebuke from her!

In the choice of colors she left me to my own taste. I was pleased with an outline of yellow upon a background of dark blue, or a combination of red and myrtle-green. There was another of red with a bluish-gray that was more conventionally used. When I became a little familiar with designing and the various pleasing combinations of color, a harder lesson was given me. It was the sewing on, instead of beads, some tinted porcupine quills, moistened and flattened between the nails of the thumb and forefinger. My mother cut off the prickly ends and burned them at once in the center fire. These sharp points were poisonous, and worked into the flesh wherever they lodged. For this reason, my mother said, I should not do much alone in quills until I was as tall as my cousin Warca-Ziwin.

Always after these confining lessons I was wild with surplus spirits, and found joyous relief in running loose in the open again. Many a summer afternoon, a party of four or five of my playmates roamed over the hills with me. We each carried a light sharpened rod about four feet long, with which we pried up certain sweet roots. When we had eaten all the choice roots we chanced upon, we shouldered our rods and strayed off into patches of a stalky plant under whose yellow blossoms we found little crystal drops of gum. Drop by drop we gathered this nature's rock-candy, until each of us could boast of a lump the size of a small bird's egg. Soon satiated with its woody flavor, we tossed away our gum, to return again to the sweet roots.

I remember well how we used to exchange our necklaces, beaded belts, and sometimes even our moccasins. We pretended to offer them as gifts to one another. We delighted in impersonating our own mothers. We talked of things we had heard them say in their conversations. We imitated their various manners, even to the inflection of their voices. In the lap of the prairie we seated ourselves upon our feet, and leaning our painted cheeks in the palms of our hands, we rested our elbows on our knees, and bent forward as old women were most accustomed to do.

While one was telling of some heroic deed recently done by a near relative, the rest of us listened attentively, and exclaimed in undertones, "Han! han!" (yes! yes!) whenever the speaker paused for breath, or sometimes for our sympathy. As the discourse became more thrilling, according to our ideas, we raised our voices in these interjections. In these impersonations our parents were led to say only those things that were in common favor.

No matter how exciting a tale we might be rehearsing, the mere shifting of a cloud shadow in the landscape nearby was sufficient to change our impulses; and soon we were all chasing the great shadows that played among the hills. We shouted and whooped in the chase; laughing and calling to one another, we were like little sportive nymphs on that Dakota sea of rolling green.

On one occasion I forgot the cloud shadow in a strange notion to catch up with my own shadow. Standing straight and still, I began to glide after it, putting out one foot cautiously. When, with the greatest care, I set my foot in advance of myself, my shadow crept onward too. Then again I tried it; this time with the other foot. Still again my shadow escaped me. I began to run; and away flew my shadow, always just a step beyond me. Faster and faster I ran, setting my teeth and clenching my fists, determined to overtake my own fleet shadow. But ever swifter it glided before me, while I was growing breathless and hot. Slackening my speed, I was greatly vexed that my shadow should check its pace also. Daring it to the utmost, as I thought, I sat down upon a rock imbedded in the hillside.

So! My shadow had the impudence to sit down beside me!

Now my comrades caught up with me, and began to ask why I was running away so fast.

"Oh, I was chasing my shadow! Didn't you ever do that?" I inquired, surprised that they should not understand.

They planted their moccasined feet firmly upon my shadow to stay it, and I arose. Again my shadow slipped away, and moved as often as I did. Then we gave up trying to catch my shadow.

Before this peculiar experience I have no distinct memory of having recognized any vital bond between myself and my own shadow. I never gave it an afterthought.

Returning our borrowed belts and trinkets, we rambled homeward. That evening, as on other evenings, I went to sleep over my legends.

1. Read the following summary notes that are based on the events in "The Beadwork." These summary notes are out of order and should be rearranged in chronological order, according to the order in which they happened in the story. Number each sentence in the correct chronological order, where 1 represents the first event that occurred out of all these events and 9 represents the last event that occurred out of all these events. Write the numbers in the box next to each sentence.

☐ Zitkala-Sa and her friends search for little crystal drops of gum.

☐ Zitkala-Sa and her friends pretend to trade personal items.

☐ Mother begins her beadwork after breakfast.

☐ Zitkala-Sa and her friends pretend to be their mothers.

☐ Zitkala-Sa and her friends return one another's borrowed items and go home.

☐ Zitkala-Sa and her friends search for sweet roots, which they harvest with rods.

☐ Zitkala-Sa and her friends tell exciting stories.

☐ Zitkala-Sa tries to catch her shadow.

☐ Zitkala-Sa observes her mother's designs for her daughter's moccasins.

2. This question has two parts. First, answer Part A. Then answer Part B.

Part A

Which of the following sentences best infers how Zitkala-Sa feels about her mother's beadwork?

- ○ A. She is in awe of her mother's skill.
- ○ B. She is angered by her mother's skill.
- ○ C. She wishes her mother would make her more moccasins to show off to her friends.
- ○ D. She dislikes beading with her mother because it is too difficult.

Part B

Which details from the text best support your answer to Part A? Select all that apply.

- ☐ A. "I felt the envious eyes of my playmates upon the pretty red beads decorating my feet."
- ☐ B. "The quietness of her oversight made me feel strongly responsible and dependent upon my own judgment."
- ☐ C. "My mother required of me original designs for my lessons in beading. At first I frequently ensnared many a sunny hour into working a long design."
- ☐ D. "Then I became intensely interested in her designing. With a proud, beaming face, I watched her work."

3. Which of the following is an example of children's play in this story? Select all that apply.

☐ A. "I was pleased with an outline of yellow upon a background of dark blue, or a combination of red and myrtle-green. There was another of red with a bluish-gray that was more conventionally used. When I became a little familiar with designing and the various pleasing combinations of color, a harder lesson was given me."

☐ B. "We delighted in impersonating our own mothers. We talked of things we had heard them say in their conversations. We imitated their various manners, even to the inflection of their voices. In the lap of the prairie we seated ourselves upon our feet, and leaning our painted cheeks in the palms of our hands, we rested our elbows on our knees, and bent forward as old women were most accustomed to do."

☐ C. "On one occasion I forgot the cloud shadow in a strange notion to catch up with my own shadow. Standing straight and still, I began to glide after it, putting out one foot cautiously. When, with the greatest care, I set my foot in advance of myself, my shadow crept onward too."

☐ D. "Soon after breakfast mother sometimes began her beadwork. On a bright, clear day, she pulled out the wooden pegs that pinned the skirt of our wigwam to the ground, and rolled the canvas part way up on its frame of slender poles. Then the cool morning breezes swept freely through our dwelling, now and then wafting the perfume of sweet grasses from newly burnt prairie."

Section 7

(You must respond to all the tasks in this section before you can move on to the next section.)

Directions: A student is writing a narrative for English class. Read the student's narrative below, and then respond to tasks 1 and 2.

> A woman entered the lobby. She had a scar on her forehead. She wore a skirt and a blouse. Her hair was red. She had perfume on. She looked around. She was carrying a bag. She turned to me and said, "Where is room 1120?" Her voice was worried. Her eyes were kind. I said, "Eleventh floor—to your left." Just then the elevator doors opened.

1. Revise this narrative so as to fix structural issues and also to create a more exciting mood by adding sensory images and specific language. Write your answer in the box below.

2. Focusing on the narrator, write a paragraph that might have begun this story.

Section 8

(You must respond to all the tasks in this section before you can move on to the next section.)

Directions: A student is writing a persuasive essay for class. Read the student's essay below, and then respond to tasks 1-5.

School Uniforms Help Students

Can what you wear to school affect your education? More and more people think school uniforms improve students' learning experience and increase safety for everyone on campus. There are many types of school uniforms, ranging from outfits that look like business suits, with blazers, ties, and slacks, to something more casual, like polo shirts and khaki trousers. What they all have in common is that they replace free choice for students, but is that so bad?

The school uniform creates a sense that students are a team. This mindset can be advantageous as it means students are working together to learn. It also discourages the idea of any one person being a superstar or a loser. If a student doesn't feel like he belongs, the uniform can help him fit in. Wearing a uniform allows students to focus on their schoolwork instead of on their social status.

Many schools have adopted school uniforms to create a more level playing field for poor students. Often fashion trends are influenced by heavy marketing, whose target is to get students to buy expensive clothing and shoes. This puts unnecessary pressure on some lower-income families who can't afford to keep up with the trends. Being fashionable has absolutely no place in obtaining an education. More and more schools agree with that statement. About 50 percent of cities where lower-class students go to school require uniforms, and that number is rising. Ninety-five percent of New Orleans students wear uniforms to school every day because 39 percent of their children live below the poverty line, which is 17 points higher than the national average. School uniforms are helping New Orleans parents make sending their kids to school a bit more affordable.

Another reason why schools have adopted uniforms is to help protect students and teachers. Students wearing baggy clothes can hide dangerous objects too easily. In areas where there are a lot of gangs, the school uniforms prevent students from displaying gang colors. People often try to steal one another's high-priced fashion items. Eliminating these dangers by mandating the use of school uniforms helps students and teachers feel safer.

Free choice is not always a good thing. Some critics of uniforms argue that self-expression suffers and that free choice allows students to experiment with who they are and who they might become. While this might be true for a few students, most people will tell you that students are more likely to copy one another, following trends, than to branch out and develop a sense of self. If a student does feel like he needs to express himself through clothing, he can do it after school or on the weekends. Some schools even allow some flexibility with hair styles or accessory choices. Many students struggle to get ready in the morning and choosing what to wear can really slow down the morning routine. A school uniform certainly helps with the decision-making process.

It may take some time for students who are used to free choice to adjust to wearing a uniform, but those students will soon find that a uniform takes away a lot of the social stress students experience and allows for a more common experience. Economic issues are lessened, and safety increases. The entire school works more like a team toward the goal of educating everyone who attends.

(Data obtained from "New Orleans Kids, Working Parents, and Poverty," by Vicki Mack. *Nonprofit Knowledge Works*, last updated February 26, 2015. www.datacenterresearch.org/reports_analysis/new-orleans-kids-working-parents-and-poverty/)

1. Reread the following excerpt from this persuasive essay.

"Another reason why schools have adopted uniforms is to help protect students and teachers. Students wearing baggy clothes can hide dangerous objects too easily. In areas where there are a lot of gangs, the school uniforms prevent students from displaying gang colors. People often try to steal one another's high-priced fashion items. Eliminating these dangers by mandating the use of school uniforms helps students and teachers feel safer."

Which of the following suggestions would improve this paragraph? Select all that apply.

☐ A. Add a transition between these sentences: "In areas where there are a lot of gangs, the school uniforms prevent students from displaying gang colors." and "People try to steal one another's high-priced fashion items."

☐ B. Include evidence to show that the lack of uniforms led to dangerous behaviors at several schools

☐ C. Explain which colors belong to which gangs

☐ D. Include evidence to show national crime statistics

2. Reread the following excerpt from this persuasive essay.

"Many schools have adopted school uniforms to create a more level playing field for poor students. Often fashion trends are influenced by heavy marketing, whose target is to get students to buy expensive clothing and shoes. This puts unnecessary pressure on some lower-income families who can't afford to keep up with the trends. Being fashionable has absolutely no place in obtaining an education. More and more schools agree with that statement. About 50 percent of cities where lower-class students go to school require uniforms, and that number is rising. Ninety-five percent of New Orleans students wear uniforms to school every day because 39 percent of their children live below the poverty line, which is 17 points higher than the national average. School uniforms are helping New Orleans parents make sending their kids to school a bit more affordable."

This paragraph is missing which of the following?

O A. A topic sentence
O B. Supportive evidence
O C. An adequate explanation of the evidence
O D. A concluding sentence

3. Reread the following excerpt from this persuasive essay.

"Can what you wear to school affect your education? More and more people think school uniforms improve students' learning experience and increase safety for everyone on campus. There are many types of school uniforms, ranging from outfits that look like business suits, with blazers, ties, and slacks, to something more casual, like polo shirts and khaki trousers. What they all have in common is that they replace free choice for students, but is that so bad?

The school uniform creates a sense that students are a team. This mindset can be advantageous as it means students are working together to learn. It also discourages the idea of any one person being a superstar or a loser. If a student doesn't feel like he belongs, the uniform can help him fit in. Wearing a uniform allows students to focus on their schoolwork instead of on their social status."

Underline the sentence in this excerpt that should be edited to be more formal in tone.

4. This question has two parts. First answer Part A. Then answer Part B.

Part A

Which of the following is the author's claim in this persuasive essay?

○ A. "There are many types of school uniforms, ranging from outfits that look like business suits, with blazers, ties, and slacks, to something more casual, like polo shirts and khaki trousers."

○ B. "More and more people think school uniforms improve students' learning experience and increase safety for everyone on campus."

○ C. "It may take some time for students who are used to free choice to adjust to wearing a uniform, but those students will soon find that a uniform takes away a lot of the social stress students experience and allows for a more common experience."

○ D. "Many schools have adopted school uniforms to create a more level playing field for poor students."

Part B

Which details from the essay best support your answer to Part A? Select all that apply.

☐ A. "What they all have in common is that they replace free choice for students, but is that so bad?"

☐ B. "Some critics of uniforms argue that self-expression suffers and that free choice allows students to experiment with who they are and who they might become."

☐ C. "Eliminating these dangers by mandating the use of school uniforms helps students and teachers feel safer."

☐ D. "Wearing a uniform allows students to focus on their schoolwork instead of on their social status."

5. Identify and explain the author's counterargument in this persuasive essay. Write your answer in the box below.

Performance Task

Directions: The actual Performance Task will be broken into two sessions: the information-gathering session and the actual reading and writing session. During the reading and writing session, you will need to complete a few constructed-response questions and then write either an argumentative or explanatory essay or a short real or imagined narrative. The Performance Task will tell you what type of writing you will be working on. Since you are taking this test in a book, there will not be an information-gathering session. Rather, you will first read the sources and answer the constructed-response questions before writing your essay. Review the sources, the questions, and the task for the essay carefully, and be aware of how much time you have left. You should allot yourself no more than approximately 2 hours to complete the Performance Task.

Task:

Steel manufacturing has played a large part in the history of manufacturing in the United States. Making steel is dangerous work, and many steelworkers have been injured or have died in the last 160 years. The Amalgamated Association of Iron and Steel Workers (the AA), the Steel Workers Organizing Committee (SWOC), and the United Steelworkers (USW) are all unions that have sought to protect the rights of steelworkers during this time period.

How did steel mills contribute to the rise of labor unions? This is the subject of the essay you are writing for history class. In your research, you have come across a painting, two articles, and a poem.

In Part 1, you will carefully review these sources, and then you will answer some questions. Briefly scan the sources and the three questions that follow. In Part 2, you will write an explanatory essay on how steel manufacturing contributed to the rise of labor unions.

Directions:

1. Read all the sources, and take notes.

2. Answer three questions about the sources.

3. Plan and write your essay.

Part 1

Source Number 1—The Monongahela River Valley, Pennsylvania

by John Kane (1931)

The Monongahela River Valley in Pennsylvania was the site of Homestead Steel Works and other steel industry sites.

Source Number 2—A Brief History of the U.S. Steelmaking Industry

by John Stone

(The following article discusses the height of steel manufacturing in the United States.)

The Industrial Revolution in the 1800s put Europe and the United States into high production of just about everything. Manufacturing was where all the money was to be made. The Bessemer process and open hearth furnaces were introduced in England and Germany, and these two countries soon become the leaders in the steelmaking industry. The United States already had basic steel mills, but these new styles of steel production helped the United States jump into the steel industry in the mid-1880s when the Lake

Superior region opened several iron ore ranges. U.S. steel mills were quickly built by English and Irish immigrants familiar with the Bessemer designs. Andrew Carnegie started his company, Edgar Thomson Steel Works, in 1872 and quickly became a leader in the industry. His plant was used as a model design for many other plants. He became very rich, especially as he bought up smaller mills, eliminating his competition. Most of the steel produced in the 1800s was used in the construction of railroads that were newly crisscrossing the country. As a result, U.S. steel production boomed.

Work in the steel mills was very dangerous. In order to manufacture steel, iron ore, coke, and limestone are combined into the "charge" and are dumped into the furnace to be blasted with hot air. Coal must be converted to coke, which involves extracting tar and dangerous gases. When the charge is melting, toxic carbon monoxide as well as other gases escape. Once the iron is melted, impurities, called "slag," float to the top and must be poured off the top. The slag was often used to create the ballast, or the bed of rocks that the railroad tracks are laid on. Moving the coal and charge was very dusty, and those dust particles were poisonous. Breathing in that dust created a lifelong disease, called "black lung," which doctors mistakenly thought was tuberculosis at first. Coal dust was not the only deadly thing to breathe in; carbon monoxide and other hot gases were dangerous for workers' lungs. Even more frightening, those gases sometimes exploded. Another danger was the molten iron that could cause severe and deadly burns. Iron is heavy, and moving it around could be crushing if it fell on a worker. Working with it every day could also create crippling back and skeletal injuries. Many jobs required workers to crawl into small, hot, and toxic spaces to gather coal, clear ashes, or check chimneys. Children were often employed to do this sort of work and received only about a third of what their parents were paid. Workers were in danger of falling from tall heights or having hot metal splinters fly into their eyes and skin from the grinding work. Even the loud noises had the potential to create permanent hearing loss.

The early days of the steel industry were very long days—sometimes as long as 12 hours. Most people worked six days a week, though the mill was open seven days a week, 24 hours a day. Carnegie only closed the plant on the Fourth of July. The wages were not very good so many people worked extra hours to try to earn enough money to feed their families. Approximately ten dollars a week was the average salary, which put the workers barely above the $500 a year poverty line. After so many hours, workers would get sleepy and have accidents. Steel mills would often hire immigrants who worked for less money and who often received little to no training for these dangerous jobs. There were Italians, Greeks, Germans, and Poles, with a lot of other countries in the world represented as well. Many of these immigrant workers spoke limited or no English. They were usually willing to tolerate the terrible working conditions in exchange for steady paychecks. The hottest, dirtiest, and most dangerous jobs were given to the immigrants and also to African-Americans, making these individuals particularly vulnerable to accidents. With very little training, communication issues occurred, and people were injured as a result. Each year, about 25 percent of the immigrant workers were killed or injured on the job, which was double that of white Americans. Even with the poor pay and the dangerous conditions, people needed work and the steel mills needed employees, so business continued to grow.

In 1901, Carnegie sold his company to the United States Steel Corporation. The new century introduced all sorts of new inventions like automobiles and airplanes. With the invention of the elevator, and more importantly the elevator brake, skyscrapers soared upward, each one needing essential steel beams for strength. The steel industry continued growing to meet the demand for these products.

World War II (1939–1945) was especially good for the steel industry. The war effort needed boats, submarines, and weapons. The steel industry had a history of helping war efforts. During the Civil War, the early steel mills manufactured cannon balls for the Union side, and during World War II, they continued this tradition of producing the materials the war effort required, like propellers and torpedoes. Additionally, the war devastation in Europe and Japan severely damaged the European and Japanese steel-making efforts. The United States mills swooped into those markets and dominated them, making record sales. Eventually Europe and Japan were able to rebuild their plants with the latest technologies in the 1950s and the 1960s, which boosted production and left the United States in the dust. By this time, the Bessemer technology was considered old and inefficient. The newer technologies helped save money. Fortunately, in 1970, Congress passed the Occupational Safety and Health Act (OSHA), which made companies more responsible for worker safety. This act drastically helped improve working conditions.

The 1980s were even more challenging for steel companies. During some labor strikes, companies, like those in the automobile manufacturing industry, could not wait for the workers and companies to resolve disputes, so they made contracts with foreign companies and imported the steel, which crippled the U.S. steel industry. Additionally, the United States just wasn't building as much as it used to, so the domestic need for steel also decreased. The steel industry responded by revamping its production models to be more internationally competitive, and they also downsized many of their mills to be more efficient.

Today the United States continues to produce steel; however, the cheaper cost of labor in other countries creates real competition. The U.S. actually imports about 30 percent of its steel. As a result, the U.S. steel industry has never returned to the levels it saw in the first half of the 20th century.

Source Number 3—Steel Mills

by Langston Hughes

(Langston Hughes, a prominent poet of the Harlem Renaissance, wrote this poem when he was only fourteen years old.)

The Mills

That grind and grind,

That grind out steel

And grind away lives

Of men—

In the sunset their stacks

Are great black silhouettes

Against the sky.

In the dawn

They belch red fire.

Grinding out new steel,

Old men.

Source Number 4—United States Steel Labor Unions

by *SteelLaborHistory.com**

(The website *SteelLaborHistory.com* documents the history and rise of steel labor unions in the United States. *Note that this website is fictional and was created for the purpose of this exercise.)

A labor union is an organization of workers who band together to protect workers' interests. Usually they fight for safer working conditions, fair wages, or reasonable working hours. When workers unionize, they decide to act as one voice in negotiation with employers to give workers more power on the job. Union representatives are elected by the workers. Any issues or concerns that workers have are voted on, and the union representatives take those concerns to the employers. The reason why this works is because a company is not functional without its workers, so if all the workers strike, the business is crippled. Historically, workers have had to strike for their rights because companies were taking advantage of them. Companies know that workers need their jobs to provide for their families, so this puts the workers in a tough position.

In the United States, workers in many industries, like the steel industry, the textile manufacturing industry, carpentry, and many others, have worked long hours, in dangerous conditions, for very little money. Workers have gone on strike to protest, sometimes with success and sometimes without it. Early strikes were often met with angry actions from employers, who would hire security guards or temporary workers, called "scabs." Tempers would boil over, and several conflicts led to violence. Employers' security would fire into crowds or set off tear gas to disperse the protesters. Strikers would sometimes fire back, and there are a number of records of gunfights. Is a job worth your life? Some workers would return to work without their needs being addressed, while others were willing to take the bullet. The conflicts between employers and workers went back and forth for decades.

The labor unions were essential to creating lifesaving changes for workers. They often helped negotiate for higher wages, shorter hours, safer workplaces, health care, and many other benefits. Below is a time line of major events that occurred for steelworkers starting in the late 1800s and how their lives were shaped by these labor unions.

Time Line of Major Steelworker Events

Date	Event	Details	Result
1876	Amalgamated Association of Iron and Steel Workers (the AA) is formed after striking about working conditions and pay.	First union for steelworkers formed.	Workers lost the strike. As a result, many left the AA union.
1892	Homestead Steel Strike	On July 6, strikers from the Homestead Steel Mill in Pennsylvania were engaged in a daylong gun battle.	Twelve people were killed.
1909	Pressed Steel Car Strike	A walk-out lasted from July 13 through September 8. On August 22, this walk-out led to a bloody battle between security agents, Pennsylvania state police, and strikers. At least twelve people died. The strikers were protesting low and changeable wages, dangerous working conditions, and the corrupt system of stores and housing provided by the company that caused the workers to always be in debt.	Wage rates were posted, but did not increase. Housing continued to be poor, and inflated pricing at the company store continued.
1910	Bethlehem Steel Strike	This was a one hundred and eight-day strike. Workers wanted Sundays off and to dissolve the "bonus" system that forced workers to work overtime.	The strikers lost.
1910	Accident Reports Act was passed in Congress	Steelworkers and other laborers lobbied for this act to make the workday more reasonable and to help create safer working conditions.	This act led to a ten-hour workday.
1915	Youngstown, Ohio Steel Strike	Five hundred workers went on strike for higher wages. Other workers then joined to form 16,000 protesters. On January 7, company guards fired on the crowd. Gunfights continued. Three died, and 125 were injured.	Workers' wages increased from 19.5 cents to 20 cents an hour.

Date	Event	Details	Result
Sept. 1919 to Jan. 1920	Great Steel Strike ("Women's Massacre")	Three hundred and fifty thousand steelworkers went on strike, and half of the steel mills shut down. Workers wanted higher pay and safer working conditions. Workers were attacked by the employers with tear gas. A gunfight broke out.	This strike failed.
1935	Wagner Act was passed in Congress	Also called the National Labor Relations Act, the Wagner Act protects workers, allowing them to form unions and engage in collective bargaining. This act also protects workers' right to strike.	Unions were protected as a result of this act.
1936	Steel Workers Organizing Committee (SWOC) forms	SWOC eventually becomes United Steelworkers (USW).	Through mergers and alliances, the USW became the largest labor union in North America.
1937	Little Steel Strike	Workers wanted a pay scale of $5 a day, an eight-hour work day, and health benefits. They wanted time and a half pay for working overtime. This was one of the most violent strikes. Workers demonstrated at a sit-in to discourage employers from simply hiring "scabs" to replace striking workers and ignoring workers' demands. This strike lasted five months.	This strike failed.
1937	Memorial Day Massacre	This massacre was part of the "Little Steel Strike."	Police killed ten people and severely injured approximately another thirty through clubbing and other forms of aggression. However, SWOC gained greater power as a result of this event.
1941	Bethlehem Steel Strike	This was a four-day strike protesting the Employee Representation Plan, which was an internal union that did not have any wage-negotiating ability.	Strikers were able to join SWOC.

Date	Event	Details	Result
1952	Steel Strike of 1952	This was a fifty-three-day strike for higher wages.	Wages stayed more or less the same.
1959	Steel Strike of 1959	The steel industry was reporting record high profits. Five hundred thousand steelworkers went on strike. This strike affected many industries, like the automobile manufacturing industry.	Workers won minimum wage increases. Other industries sought contracts with foreign steel manufacturers, which permanently injured the U.S. steel market.
1970	The Occupational Safety and Health Act (OSHA) passes Congress	The OSHA was passed on December 30.	This act makes employers responsible for safe working conditions.
1986–1987	Steel Strike of 1986–1987	From August 1 to January 31, 22,000 workers were either locked out or went on strike, depending on different firsthand accounts of this event. This was the longest steel industry shutdown in U.S. history. The employers wanted to reduce pay because the industry wasn't doing well.	This strike led to renegotiated contracts to maintain pay rates.

Constructed-Response Tasks

1. What were the dangers that steelworkers faced in the steel mills? Write your answer in the box below.

2. List the improved working conditions that were won by steelworkers' unions.
   Write your answer in the box below.

3. What is a union, and why does it strike? Write your answer in the box below.

Part 2

Now review your notes and sources, and then plan, draft, and revise your essay. You may use your notes and refer back to the sources.

Your Assignment:

Write an essay for your history class that explains how the history of steel mills contributed to the rise of labor unions. Be sure to include support in your essay with details from the sources that you read and reviewed.

Explanatory Essay Scoring:

Your explanatory essay will be scored using the following:

1. **Organization/Purpose:** How well did you state your claim and maintain your claim with a logical progression of ideas from beginning to end? How well did you use transitions to explain your ideas? How effective were your introduction and your conclusion?

2. **Evidence/Elaboration:** How well did you use relevant and specific information from the sources? How well did you elaborate on your ideas? How well did you clearly state ideas in your own words? How well did you cite references to the sources you used?

3. **Conventions:** How well did you follow the rules for punctuation, capitalization, and spelling?

Now begin work on your essay. Manage your time carefully so that you have time to:

> Plan your essay
> Write your essay
> Revise and edit for a final draft

Use the work space below, and additional scratch paper if needed, to write your essay.

(Answers are on page 169.)

Answers Explained

Chapter 1: Selected-Response Tasks

Exercise 1 (pages 20–22)

1. **(B)** The word "first" is a clue that this sentence should be early in the order to establish the controlling idea ("setting a realistic goal"). The following sentences support and elaborate on the controlling idea. "Running a 5K race" is the first example. The fact that five kilometers is "not very far" expands on the idea of forming a "realistic" plan. The next sentence provides details about how that goal fits with most doctors' recommendation to get in at least 30 minutes of cardio exercise *and* continues with the thought that a 5K race is easy to complete. In the other answer choices, the supporting sentences come before the controlling idea sentence so the supporting sentences cannot expand upon the controlling idea.

2. **(C)** "Running isn't hard at all if you start smart and make a plan" captures the main point of this essay. Kevin provides several sentences that support this idea. He first describes how to start simple, and then he suggests making a plan to increase the running goal a little at a time. The last sentence of the essay reinforces this claim, too. By setting a goal and making a plan, it is easier to establish these healthy habits and stick to them.

3. **(A)** The best synonym for "*reinforcement* system" is "*reward* system," as these mean exactly the same thing: a system to reinforce positive behavior with rewards. "Strength," choice (B), is meant to fool you if you didn't know what "reinforcement" meant in this context. Although "reinforce" means "to strengthen" in some contexts, the next sentence shows that this system is built around rewards, such as treating yourself to a new pair of running socks as a reward for running three kilometers. While it might seem like a "*reinforcement* system" is trying to persuade you to keep running, "persuasive" is not an actual synonym for "reinforcement." "Dual" is an absurd answer choice that you should easily eliminate.

Exercise 2 (pages 23–24)

1. **(D)** Choices (A), (B), and (C) are all correct solutions to the comma splice found in the underlined sentence. Choice (D) is missing a comma between "soon" and "so." Just adding the conjunction word "so" cannot connect two independent clauses. You must use a conjunction and a comma together.

2. **(A)** If someone wants to hire Maria to walk his dog, there is no way to contact her because there is no phone number. All the other choices have information that can be asked over the phone, but not if she doesn't give her phone number first.

Exercise 3 (pages 25–27)

1. **(B)** This poem is about children pretending to make a ship out of furniture on the stairs and "sailing" in the nursery. The poem retells the adventure of this game, which seems to be a fond memory for the poet. "And had the very best of plays" best captures the message of the poem. The other answer choices only provide details from the poem, but these details do not capture the poet's overall message, which is that one of his fondest memories was pretending to sail in a ship with Tom when they were younger.

2. **(D)** The first line of this poem should provide you with a lot of information to help you determine the point of view that this poem is most likely told from. "We built a ship upon the stairs" contains two clues. "We" indicates that the speaker was part of the action, and "built" indicates that these events occurred in the past. Additionally, "we sailed along for days and days" indicates that these events occurred over a longer period of time (for "days and days"). Choice (A) is incorrect because it states that the point of view is that of a parent watching children play. This does not correspond with the use of "we," which indicates that the speaker participated in the action. Choice (B) is incorrect for the same reason since the nursery nanny is "observing," not participating. Choice (C) correctly indicates that the speaker is participating, but it uses the wrong tense. The speaker is not currently playing; he is reminiscing about the past. Of all the choices offered, choice (D) correctly indicates that the speaker participated in the action and that this action took place in the past (when he was a child).

Chapter 2: Technology-Enhanced Tasks

Exercise 1 (pages 33–35)

1. **(C)** The best synonym for "dominant" is "central." The word "sleepy" is obviously wrong. However, "dormant" is a synonym for sleeping, and, if you

were skimming too quickly, you may have confused "dormant" with "dominant." "Common" is also incorrect. While poor pitching may be a frequent problem for the team, the word "dominant" stresses that this problem is so severe that it is their main or central issue. "Minor" would completely alter the meaning of the sentence. If poor pitching is their least concerning problem, then what is their biggest problem? Clearly, if revising the pitching strategy was the only solution that finally led to their winning streak, then the poor pitching was the leading or central issue for the team.

2. **Franklin divided the thing or idea into its parts. Franklin listed the features of these parts. Franklin examined the connections, or relationships, among the parts. Franklin examined the connections, or relationships, between each part and the whole. Franklin made a new plan.** This task asks you to reorder the events in the order in which they occurred (chronological order). It also asks you to abstractly analyze Franklin's thinking. You will need to read the sentences and match them to the different parts of the passage. On the computerized test, you would be able to jot down notes about these connections on your notepad. Once you have matched the sentences to their respective parts of the passage, you can then untangle the order of the events and reorder the sentences accordingly.

Franklin divided the thing or idea into its parts.	"First, he listed the game's several parts: pitching, batting, fielding, and base running."
Franklin listed the features of these parts.	"offense" and "defense"
Franklin examined the connections, or relationships, among the parts.	"He realized the team was doing very well with offense. The team was batting and base running well. However, he realized that they were having a hard time with defense. The fielders were doing a great job, but the pitchers were struggling."
Franklin examined the connections, or relationships, between each part and the whole.	"Poor pitching was the dominant problem for the team."
Franklin made a new plan.	"Franklin decided to recruit a new pitcher and coached the other pitchers on some pitching techniques."

Exercise 2 (page 36)

1. **OK** and **nice** The task asks you to search for words that could be more descriptive. "OK" could be replaced with a number of improved adjectives, such as "riveting" or "entertaining." Clearly, the author of the paragraph found the movie very engaging, and the fact that the first sentence ends with an exclamation point indicates that a more positive review of the movie would better describe the author's overall positive movie-going experience. Similarly, "nice" does very little to show the writer's opinion of the music. Stronger adjectives may vary but could include "pleasant" or "enjoyable." Since the rest of the paragraph is much clearer with descriptive adjectives such as "hysterical" and "extreme," revising the weaker adjectives ("OK" and "nice") would make the paragraph even stronger.

2. **"Sarah loved to play with an old, filthy doll."** and **"Sarah traveled everywhere with Maria, which had soiled the doll considerably."** "She received it from her grandmother when she was five-years-old" has a major issue. The syntax of the sentence suggests that the grandmother gave Sarah the doll when the grandmother was five-years-old, not when Sarah was five-years-old, which is the true meaning of this sentence. The antecedent to the second "she" is "grandmother" because it was the last subject preceding the pronoun. "It had straight black hair Sarah named the doll Maria" is a run-on sentence. A period should be placed after "hair" to create two complete sentences. Additionally, a comma should separate "straight" and "black." "After her grandmother" is a fragment. "Washing the doll would be very challenged because of how fragile the doll had become" has an incorrect verb form. "Challenged" should be changed to "challenging."

Exercise 3 (pages 37–39)

1. **metaphor**, **simile**, **personification**, and **alliteration** A "metaphor" describes one thing by describing another in comparison without using "like" or "as." "He stirred his velvet head" is a metaphor because the narrator compares the bird's head to velvet fabric without the use of "like" or "as." This helps the reader think of the bird's head as soft like velvet. An "allegory" is a short moral tale. This poem does not constitute an allegory. A "simile" is very similar to a "metaphor," but it describes the comparison between two things by using "like" or "as." When the narrator states that the bird's rapid eyes "looked like frightened beads," comparing the bird's eyes to "frightened beads" is a simile. The phrase

"frightened beads" also exemplifies "personification." "Personification" gives human characteristics to inanimate objects. In this case, the beads are not living, yet they feel "frightened." "Hyperbole" is an exaggeration. There are no exaggerations in this poem. Most of the poem is very literal. There are several examples of "alliteration" in this poem. "Alliteration" is when two or more words start with the same letter consecutively; however, these sounds do not have to be back to back. In this poem, "Too silver for a seam" and "Or butterflies, off banks of noon" are examples of alliteration.

2. **"Like one in danger; cautious, / I offered him a crumb, / And he unrolled his feathers / And rowed him softer home" (Lines 13–16)**
   In these lines, the bird becomes aware of the observing speaker, and this happens at the exact moment that the observer offers him a crumb. There is a sense of tension and danger in this moment, as both are cautious of one another. This is the tensest moment in the poem, and thus it can be argued that these lines constitute a climax (the peak of the action) of the poem.

Chapter 3: Constructed-Response Tasks

Exercise 1—Narrative Response (pages 49-50)

Answers will vary. Below are sample 2-point, 1-point, and 0-point responses.

2 Points	This response:	
	> uses vivid multisensory descriptions (sights, smells, touches, etc.) > continues with same mood and situation from the stimulus text (it doesn't go off-track) > uses and develops details from the stimulus text	All the family's favorite recipes were marked with bent corners or bookmarks. Years of spills and use had greased the pages so some had become partially transparent. As Samantha carefully turned the pages, dried batter flaked into her lap, and she remembered the sweet smell of chocolate brownies that would welcome her home from her first day of school each year. She could picture her mother standing at the stove in her green apron, endlessly stirring pots.

1 Point	This response: > uses very few sensory descriptions > uses vague references to the mood and/or situation from the stimulus text	Samantha really liked her mother's cooking and wanted to cook something that would taste just as flavorful as her mother's cooking did. She didn't have any ingredients, though.
0 Points	This response: > does not use sensory descriptions > does not refer to any part of the mood and/or situation from the stimulus text	I am hungry. I wish I could eat a sandwich right now.

Exercise 2—Explanatory Response (pages 51–54)

Answers will vary. Below are sample 2-point, 1-point, and 0-point responses.

2 Points	This response: > provides an adequate conclusion that follows from and supports the preceding information in the body of writing as a whole or provides a "so what" statement (an answer as to why the information in the rest of the text is important or what should happen next) > does more than restate the points/reasons from the text—it is not formulaic > provides adequate connections and/or a progression of ideas that contributes to coherence	Steinbeck never did fully recover from the loss of his dear friend, but he did continue to write. *East of Eden* (1952) and *Travels with Charley* (1962) were two of Steinbeck's more famous books written after Ricketts' death. During his lifetime, Steinbeck published dozens of books, both fiction and nonfiction. He died in New York City in 1968. Today, Steinbeck's books continue to be widely read and are often required reading in many schools around the world. It is a shame that he did not enjoy his success as much as the world has enjoyed his books.

1 Point	This response: › provides a limited conclusion that is related to the information in the body of writing as a whole › lists, restates, or summarizes the points and reasons from the text—it is formulaic	John Steinbeck wrote two famous books, *East of Eden* (1952) and *Travels with Charley* (1962). He wrote many fiction and nonfiction books. His books are read all over the world. He died in 1968.
0 Points	This response: › provides no conclusion or a conclusion that is minimally related to the information in the body of writing as a whole › may restate random and/or incorrect details from the preceding information from the text › does not provide connections or a progression of ideas	John Steinbeck died in 1968. He wrote a lot of books that are used in schools all over the world.

Exercise 3—Argumentative Response (pages 55–58)

Answers will vary. Below are sample 2-point, 1-point, and 0-point responses.

2 Points	This response: › provides adequate supporting arguments and/or relevant evidence based on the given arguments from the text › does more than list supporting arguments › develops an adequate counterargument(s) › adequately elaborates arguments using precise words and language	Throughout time, humans have invented technology that enhances their life experiences. The technology today is especially good at helping teenagers manage their busy lives. Teens struggle to balance home life, sports practice, homework, part-time jobs, and academics, and any teen would say that their friendships are extremely important to them as well. But how can they balance it all? Technology. Text messages, video chats, and the extensive Internet enrich teenagers' social

2 Points (cont'd)

experiences. Having a bad day isn't as bad when a person can reach out to a friend for a quick virtual hug and a bit of encouragement. It can instantly feel like having a person in your corner. Felipe argues that "a text is not a substitute for a hug," but friends can't always be there in person. An encouraging emoji can help until a friend can give the in-person hug. Felipe seems to be arguing that technology should not replace in-person friendships. Teens aren't replacing in-person friendships, but they are using technology to add to their experiences. Technology is helping teens communicate more effectively and more frequently. It is awkward being a teenager, especially if the person feels like he or she is different from everyone else. Sofia seems to understand the difficulties that some teens experience when making friends if they feel odd or out of place. People who feel less connected can "[meet] friends through fan pages or in an online game," and this can be a lifesaver for people who struggle with their immediate social circles. It is true that "people can exaggerate or outright lie very easily" when online, as Felipe argues, but most people will say that those experiences do not only happen online. Middle schools and high schools may contain people who are not always honest and upfront. Being a teenager is about figuring out how to be true to oneself, regardless of the forum. It takes experimentation and the development of true friendships to do this. Technology can really help with that experience.

1 Point	This response: > provides mostly general and/or limited supporting arguments and/or relevant evidence, which may be extraneous or loosely related > lists supporting arguments with limited elaboration/evidence > partially develops a counterargument(s) > partially elaborates arguments using general words/language	Technology can really help teens stay connected to one another. Text messages, video chats, and the extensive Internet enrich teenagers' social experiences. Felipe argues that texts "cause many fights and hurt feelings." An encouraging emoji can help until a friend can give the in-person hug. It is awkward being a teenager, especially if the person feels like he or she is different from everyone else. People who feel less connected can "[meet] friends through fan pages or in an online game." People who are popular and those who are not popular can have friends the same way. Technology can really help with that experience.
0 Points	This response: > provides minimal or no supporting arguments and/or relevant evidence based on the given arguments > provides supporting arguments and/or evidence that may be unclear, repetitive, incorrect, contradictory to, or interfering with the meaning of the stimulus text > does not develop a counterargument(s) > provides no appropriate elaboration and/or may use poor word choice	Technology helps teens have their friendships. They can talk about their feelings or talk about anything they want. What if you are mad at someone? Write a text. You text whatever you want about their feelings. Felipe thinks that people just text to hurt feelings, but he is wrong. Teens text emojis, pictures, and anything. Sofia is more right about how teens use our screens. We need our technology now!

Chapter 4: Performance Task Overview

Backpacks Performance Task (pages 85–95)

Part 1

1. **Answers will vary. Below are sample 2-point, 1-point, and 0-point responses.**

2 Points	This response: > clearly demonstrates an understanding of the prompt > demonstrates an understanding of the stimulus text > uses details from the stimulus text	When a student carries a backpack that is heavier than 10 percent of the student's weight, the bulk can create physical problems. According to the National Safety Council, a child carrying a backpack that is too heavy may be prone to "bending forward" while wearing the backpack, and he or she may complain about "tingling or numbness." The National Safety Council also cautions that carrying a heavy load can "cause a lot of problems for kids, like back and shoulder pain, and poor posture." Students can avoid permanent health issues by carrying a lighter backpack.
1 Point	This response: > demonstrates some understanding of the prompt and the stimulus text > uses vague references to the stimulus text	When a student carries a heavy backpack, he or she might have physical problems like back problems. Students should carry lighter backpacks.
0 Points	This response: > does not demonstrate an understanding of the prompt and the stimulus text > does not refer to any part of the stimulus text	Backpacks hurt students.

2. **Answers will vary. Below are sample 2-point, 1-point, and 0-point responses.**

2 Points	This response: > clearly demonstrates an understanding of the prompt > demonstrates an understanding of the stimulus text > uses details from the stimulus text	In her article, "25 Terrible Things About Lockers," Shivani suggests that students sometimes hesitate to use lockers for a variety of reasons. Lockers are often the wrong shape or are often in the wrong location of the school. Items such as "lacrosse sticks" never fit correctly and always "get stuck" in the lockers. Sometimes a student will have "a locker on the opposite end of the school" from his or her friends' lockers, and the student will prefer to spend time socializing at his or her friend's locker rather than traveling to another part of the school to use his or her own locker. The wear and tear on lockers throughout the years also takes a toll, making them smell bad or break and rust. Other students find that "opening the lock is basically impossible."
1 Point	This response: > demonstrates some understanding of the prompt and the stimulus text > uses vague references to the stimulus text	Students might not want to use lockers because they are too far away, and they can't use them to store things like lacrosse sticks. They might also want to hang out with their friends. Plus, lockers get broken a lot.
0 Points	This response: > does not demonstrate an understanding of the prompt and the stimulus text > doesn't refer to any part of the stimulus text	Lockers squeak a lot when you open them.

3. **Answers will vary. Below are sample 2-point, 1-point, and 0-point responses.**

2 Points	This response: > clearly demonstrates an understanding of the prompt > demonstrates an understanding of the stimulus text > uses details from the stimulus text	Students may wish to bring backpacks to class rather than using their lockers for two key reasons. Students may stay more organized when they have all of their books in their backpacks, arranged the way they want them in the order they will need them. Lockers are also frequently vandalized, and there are "several locker break-ins" in some schools in which locked items are at risk and "students' stuff has been strewn all about." ("Which Backpacks Fit Into Lockers?") Wearing a backpack to class allows students to have all of their required materials in their possession, and a backpack stores all of these items safely.
1 Point	This response: > demonstrates some understanding of the prompt and the stimulus text > uses vague references to the stimulus text	Students like to stay organized by wearing a backpack and keeping things in it. Stuff gets stolen in lockers.
0 Points	This response: > does not demonstrate an understanding of the prompt and the stimulus text > doesn't refer to any part of the stimulus text	I like to use a red backpack and wear it only on one shoulder.

Part 2

Answers will vary. Below are sample criteria for 4-point, 3-point, 2-point, 1-point, and NS (No Score) responses.

Argumentative Score: 4	
Organization/Purpose	This response has a clear and effective organizational structure that creates a sense of unity and completeness. The organization is fully sustained between and within paragraphs. This response is consistently and purposefully focused. > A claim is introduced and clearly communicated, and the focus is strongly maintained for the purpose and audience. > There is consistent use of a variety of transitional strategies to clarify the relationships between and among ideas. There is also an effective introduction and conclusion. > There is a logical progression of ideas from beginning to end. There are strong connections between and among ideas with some syntactic variety. > Alternate and opposing arguments are clearly acknowledged or addressed.
Evidence/Elaboration	This response provides thorough and convincing elaboration of the support/evidence for the claim and argument(s) including reasoned, in-depth analysis and the effective use of source material. This response clearly and effectively develops ideas, using precise language. > Comprehensive evidence (facts and details) from the source material is integrated, relevant, and specific. > There are clear citations or attributions to the source material. > There is effective use of a variety of elaborative techniques (which may include the use of personal experiences that support the argument). > The vocabulary is clearly appropriate for the audience and purpose. > An effective, appropriate style enhances the content.
Conventions Score: 2	
This response demonstrates an adequate command of conventions and an adequate use of correct sentence formation, punctuation, capitalization, grammar usage, and spelling.	

Every day across this great nation, hundreds of students head off to school with backpacks filled with books, tablets, paper, and other supplies they need for the day. While backpacks are a much-needed accessory for students, they can be harmful to the student's health. Regular use of backpacks can cause back problems, bad posture, and prolonged aches and pains. They also create other hazards in the classroom. Students should not be allowed to bring backpacks to class because they cause health issues, create safety problems, and distract students from paying attention in class.

Students should not wear backpacks to class because they cause a number of health issues. According to the National Safety Council, "backpacks that are too heavy can cause a lot of problems for kids, like back and shoulder pain, and poor posture" ("Backpack Safety: It's Time to Lighten the Load"). Their fragile bodies are still developing and carrying heavy backpacks can actually hurt students. Students should not jeopardize their health just because they are too lazy to stop at their lockers or because they want to visit with their friends and that takes up the time they would be stopping at their lockers. In her article, "25 Terrible Things About Lockers," Shivani argues that students are often assigned lockers far from their friends' lockers. However, she neglects to explain how this is true for most students. Furthermore, students can visit with friends before and after school and at lunch. Students shouldn't use up their time to drop off books in their lockers to chat with friends. Two minutes of chatting with a friend between classes isn't worth all the back and neck pain that will result from failing to drop off your books at your locker and instead carrying them around in your backpack all day.

The American Chiropractic Association published information to help parents understand the health problems for students. They recommend "a full backpack weigh no more than 10 percent of a child's weight" ("Backpack Safety: It's Time to Lighten the Load"). In other words, if a student weighs 100 pounds, his backpack shouldn't weigh more than ten pounds. A science text, a history text, and a multiple-section binder can easily total ten pounds, so lugging all of his or her textbooks around all day will certainly affect a student's health. Carrying backpacks around to all classes can make this problem even worse. Some argue that backpacks with wheels may solve the issue. However, others note that "part of the reason [those backpacks are] so heavy [is] due to the fact that [they have] wheels and a handle" ("Which Backpacks Fit Into Lockers"). With all of the added weight caused by regular backpacks and backpacks with wheels, it only makes sense to ban them during the school day and instead encourage students to use their lockers effectively.

When students wear backpacks to class, they also create a safety hazard for their teachers and classmates. Some classrooms can be overcrowded, and each backpack creates more chaos. In the blog post entitled "Which Backpacks Fit Into Lockers," one parent argues this point, stating that "there is no room in many classrooms for the two backpacks plus the musical instruments many students carry around school. All these backpacks take up too much space, and teachers complained that people were tripping over them." It's true that students rarely tuck their backpacks into safe locations, but instead leave them in the aisles and strewn about. In an emergency, this would be a critical life-threatening exit issue, but even in everyday situations, "they clutter school corridors, replacing a potential back injury hazard with a tripping hazard" ("Backpack Safety: It's Time to Lighten the Load"). Additionally, students might steal things such as a science microscope, which can be expensive to replace, and hide them in their backpacks. Some people argue that lockers aren't any safer than backpacks because students break into one another's lockers. However, this is often because the student didn't lock his locker properly or because he gave his friends his combination ("Which Backpacks Fit Into Lockers?"). Therefore, if a student is vigilant about locking his locker, then keeping his books in his locker is much safer than carrying them around all day and risk causing physical injuries or possibly losing any of his belongings.

Backpacks are also full of items that students will likely use to distract themselves from learning. Teachers forbid students from using cell phones and eating snacks in class, but those warnings usually don't work. Students might pull their phones out of their backpacks to take pictures of tests or text the answers back and forth, compromising their integrity. A student wanting to sneak a quick snack from his backpack is preoccupied with hiding the noise and chewing from the teacher when she is turned away, so that the student is actually missing an opportunity to learn. If the student just ate the snack at brunch or lunch, he would be able to concentrate on the lesson. What else is in the backpack? Beyond cell phones and snacks, students bring all sorts of distractions, like games. If one student pulls something like that out, it distracts all the students who either want to share it, just watch the student play with it, or are just distracted by all the whispering and commotion surrounding the contraband. In order to help students concentrate on the lessons, they should not be tempted by the distractions that backpacks offer.

Students may be annoyed at first by the new backpack ban, but they will ultimately be rewarded. Tripping hazards will be reduced. Crime on campus may decrease. Students will be able to stand taller and with less pain. Fewer toys and electronics will find their way into class. Students will be forced to organize their belongings more thoughtfully instead of constantly dumping more items into their backpacks. Since backpacks cause health issues, create safety problems, and distract students from paying attention in class, they should not be allowed in classrooms.

Argumentative Score: 3	
Organization/Purpose	This response has an evident organizational structure and a sense of completeness. Though there may be minor flaws, they do not interfere with the overall coherence. The organization is adequately sustained between and within paragraphs. This response is generally focused. › A claim is clear, and the focus is mostly maintained for the purpose and audience. › There is an adequate use of transitional strategies with some variety to clarify relationships between and among ideas. There is also an adequate introduction and conclusion. › There is an adequate progression of ideas from beginning to end. There are adequate connections between and among ideas. › Alternate and opposing arguments are adequately acknowledged or addressed.
Evidence/Elaboration	This response provides an adequate elaboration of the support/evidence for the claim and argument(s) including reasoned analysis and the use of source material. This response adequately develops ideas and employs a mix of precise language and more general language. › Adequate evidence (facts and details) from the source material is integrated and relevant, yet may be general. › There is an adequate use of citations or attributions to the source material. › There is an adequate use of some elaborative techniques (which may include the use of personal experiences that support the argument). › The vocabulary is generally appropriate for the audience and purpose. › A generally appropriate style is evident.

Students head off to school with backpacks filled with the supplies they need for the day, but backpacks can be harmful to their health. Regular use of backpacks can cause health problems. They also create safety issues in the classroom and can be distracting. Backpacks should not be allowed in classrooms during the day.

Students should not wear backpacks to class because they cause health issues. According to the National Safety Council, "backpacks that are too heavy can cause a lot of problems for kids, like back and shoulder pain, and poor posture" ("Backpack Safety: It's Time to Lighten the Load"). Their bodies are still developing, and carrying a backpack can hurt. Students should not jeopardize their health just because they are too lazy to stop at their lockers or because they want to visit with their friends. The best way to protect students' health is to minimize the use of backpacks during the day.

Backpacks create a safety hazard for teachers and classmates. Some classrooms can be overcrowded, and each backpack creates more chaos. "It has to do with safety issues because there is no room in many classrooms for the two backpacks plus the musical instruments many students carry around school. All these backpacks take up too much space, and teachers complained that people were tripping over them." ("Which Backpacks Fit Into Lockers?"). Students rarely tuck their backpacks into safe locations, but instead leave them in the aisles and strewn about. Additionally, students might steal things and hide them in their backpacks. Some people argue that lockers aren't any safer than backpacks because students break into one another's lockers ("Which Backpacks Fit Into Lockers?"). This argument has nothing to do with whether or not students should bring backpacks to class. Students will be much safer if they use their lockers than if they use their backpacks.

Students distract themselves from learning with what's in their backpacks. Teachers tell students not to use cell phones or eat snacks in class. Students might use the phones from their backpacks to take pictures of tests or text the answers back and forth. Students pull snacks from their backpacks, missing out on an opportunity to learn. If the student just ate the snack at brunch or lunch, he would be able to concentrate on the lesson. Students bring all sorts of distractions in their backpacks, like games. If one student pulls something like that out, people just watch the student play with it, or they are just distracted by all the whispering. Students should not be tempted by the distractions from their backpacks.

Students may be annoyed by the new backpack ban, but they will be rewarded. Tripping and crime on campus will decrease. Students will have less pain and fewer toys to distract them. Because backpacks cause health issues, create safety problems, and distract students, they should not be allowed in classrooms.

Argumentative Score: 2	
Organization/Purpose	This response has an inconsistent organizational structure. Some flaws are evident, and some ideas may be loosely connected. The organization is somewhat sustained between and within paragraphs. This response may have a minor drift in focus. > A claim may be somewhat unclear, or the focus may be insufficiently sustained for the purpose and/or audience. > There is an inconsistent use of transitional strategies and/or little variety. The introduction or conclusion, if present, may be weak. > There is an uneven progression of ideas from beginning to end that may be formulaic. There are inconsistent or unclear connections between and among ideas. > Alternate and opposing arguments may be confusing or not acknowledged.

Argumentative Score: 2	
Evidence/Elaboration	This response provides uneven, cursory elaboration of the support/evidence for the claim and argument(s) including some reasoned analysis and partial or uneven use of source material.
	> Some of the evidence (facts and details) from the source material may be weakly integrated, imprecise, repetitive, vague, and/or copied.
	> There is a weak use of citations or attributions to the source material.
	> There is a weak or uneven use of elaborative techniques (which may consist primarily of source summary and/or may rely on emotional appeal).
	> The vocabulary is uneven or somewhat ineffective for the audience and purpose.
	> There is an inconsistent or weak attempt to create appropriate style.

Conventions Score: 1
This response demonstrates a partial command of conventions and a limited use of correct sentence formation, punctuation, capitalization, grammar usage, and spelling.

Students like to put lots of stuff in their backpacks. This is not good for them. It is unsafe. Backpacks are causing a lot of problems.

Students should not wear backpacks because its not good for them. Backpacks that are to heavy can cause a lot of problems for kids like back and shoulder pain and poor posture. Students should watch out for themselves. They are to lazy to use their lockers. They just want to be with there friends. What's better: talking to your friends and carrying your books all day or putting your books away during the day and seeing your friends later?

Students should not wear backpacks because it is unsafe. Some classrooms have to much stuff. Teachers say its dangerous. Students throw their stuff everywhere. They might steal microscopes. Some people say lockers are bad cause students break into them but thats just cause they don't lock them. They will be better off if they use their lockers.

Students should not wear backpacks because it is distracting. They might text each other. Students might then want to eat in class. They might bring stuff in their backpacks to play with during class that other people will want to take.

Students will be safer and not have so much pains if they stop using backpacks.

Argumentative Score: 1	
Organization/Purpose	This response has little or no discernible organizational structure. The response may be related to the claim, but it may provide little or no focus. > A claim may be confusing or ambiguous, the response may be too brief, or the focus may drift from the purpose and/or audience. > Few or no transitional strategies are evident. An introduction and/or conclusion may be missing. > Frequent extraneous ideas may be evident. Ideas may be randomly ordered or have an unclear progression. > Alternate and opposing arguments may not be acknowledged.
Evidence/Elaboration	This response provides minimal elaboration of the support/evidence for the claim and argument(s) including little or no use of source material. This response is vague, lacks clarity, or is confusing. > The evidence (facts and details) from the source material is minimal, irrelevant, absent, incorrectly used, or predominantly copied. > There is insufficient use of citations or attributions to the source material. > There is minimal, if any, use of elaborative techniques (emotional appeal may dominate the writing). > The vocabulary used is limited or ineffective for the audience and purpose. > There is little or no evidence of appropriate style in the writing.
Conventions Score: 0	
This response demonstrates little or no command of conventions and an infrequent use of correct sentence formation, punctuation, capitalization, grammar usage, and spelling.	

Students like to put lots of stuff in their backpacks. This is not good for them. It is bad for them cause of health problems. Students should watch out for theirselves. They are to lazy to use there lockers. They just want to be with there friends. They should just use some lockers. Teachers say its bad too. Students throw their stuff everywhere. They might steal microscopes. They might text each another. One might want to eat in class. Kids just want to play. Backpacks aren't safe and are a reel pain in the neck!

Argumentative Score: NS (No Score)

> Insufficient (includes copied text)
> In a language other than English
> Off-topic
> Off-purpose

(The score "NS" is for extreme cases where a student cannot write anything close to what is expected.)

Chapter 5: Practice Test

Computer Adaptive Test (pages 97–134)

Section 1

1. **(A)** "Affluent" people are "wealthy" people. Choices (B) and (C) try to confuse you by offering answers with similar roots to "affluent"; however, neither is a close synonym of "affluent." "Influential" means "affecting" or "swaying something," while "fluent" means "spoken with ease." Choice (D) is incorrect because being "affluent" or well off financially is not the same as being "important." (1-point answer)

2. **(B)** While choices (A), (C), and (D) all capture ideas mentioned in the article, they do not capture the main message or idea of the entire article, which is that maps served several purposes in early America. Choice (A) captures some of the ideas in the second paragraph, which discusses how displaying maps was seen as a symbol of wealth and status. The last paragraph discusses the role of maps in war and how the outcome of the Revolutionary War was shifted as a result of George Washington's ability to consult a map and cross the Delaware River. Choice (D) captures the main topic explored in the fourth paragraph, which is the role that maps played in trade and business. (1-point answer)

3. **"Most businesses relied on trade, and reliable trade routes helped with their success."** This sentence is a strong topic sentence. Placing it at the beginning of this paragraph helps focus the reader on the topic being discussed in this paragraph. The rest of the sentences then flow logically after moving this sentence to the beginning of this paragraph. (1-point answer)

4. **(B)** Choice (A), "How to Have a Dinner Party with a Map," does not capture the entirety of the subject of the article; it only captures a portion of the second paragraph, which discusses how wealthy individuals would display maps as a status symbol in their dining rooms for dinner guests to admire. Only the fourth paragraph discusses the relationship between shipping and maps, so choice (C), "Without a Map, the Early Colonial Shipping Businesses Would Have Sunk," does not include enough of the article. Furthermore, it is excessively wordy for a title. Choice (D), "Mapping Early America," would indicate that the article will discuss the process of creating maps of early America, but this article discusses much more than that. Therefore, the best answer given is choice (B), "A Brief History of Maps in Early America," because it indicates the many ways maps were used in early America. (1-point answer)

5. **Answers will vary. Below are sample 2-point, 1-point, and 0-point responses.**

| 2 Points | This response:
> fully explains why hanging a map in the dining room would give the impression of intelligence
> uses strong textual evidence to support the explanation
> adequately introduces and comments on the textual evidence | Hanging a map of the American colonies or early America in one's dining room would help the person seem more intelligent to visitors. In the article "Maps," the author suggests that maps "would show their worldly and scientific interests." During this time period, many discoveries were being made by Europeans about the land in North America. Displaying a map in the home symbolized that the owner was interested in business and trade opportunities, geography, and scientific discoveries. All of these areas of interest require knowledge and imply that the owner has studied these |

		things. Therefore, this status symbol in the home would give the impression that the owner is intelligent.
1 Point	This response: > attempts to explain why hanging a map in the dining room would give the impression of intelligence > uses poor or not enough textual evidence to support the explanation > attempts to introduce and/or make commentary on the textual evidence	Hanging a map of the American colonies or early America in one's dining room might make a person seem more intelligent. The article says, "the success of the colonies, and later on the United States, was dependent on the acquisition of land," and as a result "acre-by-acre maps were drawn of the sprawling growth." Maps showed this to the dinner guests.
0 Points	This response: > does not explain why hanging a map in the dining room would give the impression of intelligence > does not use textual evidence to support the explanation	Maps were very important to wealthy people to make them look smart. They would hang them in their houses.

Section 2

1. **Answers will vary.** See below for a sample response.

The Chinese New Year Explanatory Essay Outline

I.   Introduction of the Chinese New Year celebrations

    A.   Begins a new lunar calendar

    B.   Coincides with the start of spring

    C.   Importance of the Chinese New Year celebration

II. Preparing for the Chinese New Year

    A.   Houses cleaned

    B.   Windows washed

    C.   Curtains cleaned

    D.   Brooms and brushes hidden

    E. All debts paid or reduced

    F. *Lai see*: lucky red money envelopes given to friends and family

        1. The amount of money should be in even numbers (odd numbers are associated with funerals)

    G. Offerings made in the temple to honor ancestors

    H. New clothes bought

    I. Hair is not washed, so as not to "wash away" good luck

    J. Banquets and reunions attended

    K. At midnight, doors and windows opened to let the "old year" out

III. Home decorations

    A. Branches of peaches, almonds, or apricots

    B. Pears are avoided because "separation" and "pear" are the same word in Chinese

    C. Calligraphy of "good luck" is hung

    D. Red lanterns

    E. Images of the Chinese zodiac are hung

    F. Traditional foods, including narcissus and daffodil bulbs, are prepared

    G. Fruit arrangement: oranges, kumquats, and tangerines

        1. The sweetness symbolizes a "sweet life"

IV. Chinese New Year parade

    A. Firecrackers

        1. Supposed to scare away bad spirits

    B. Cymbals, drums, and metal gongs

    C. Parade floats

    D. Lion dancers

        1. Papier-mâché head

        2. Head painted red, yellow, green, and orange

    E. Dragon

        1. Breathes real fire and smoke

        2. Zig-zags down the street

        3. Brings rainfall

        4. Symbolizes the Emperor

        5. Appears at the Chinese New Year

Note that, on the actual computerized test, you would use your mouse to drag-and-drop each item in the outline into the correct order. Your revised outline should resemble the one on pages 171–172. The introduction will include an overview of the event and its traditions. Both "Coincides with the start of spring" and "Importance of the Chinese New Year celebration" fit better in a paragraph that gives an overview of the holiday. Each item listed in the rest of this outline "coincides with the start of spring" and adds to the "importance of the Chinese New Year celebration." It does not matter if you put these two points in this order or if you reversed their order, so long as they are both listed as part of the introduction.

The "Preparing for the Chinese New Year" paragraph discusses the many traditions that occur in preparation for this holiday. One tradition is giving "*lai see*," which are "lucky red money envelopes given to friends and family." Originally, this discussion was placed in the "Chinese New Year parade" paragraph, but that does not make sense given that this is a tradition or practice, not something that occurs during a parade or festival. The description that states that "The amount of money should be in even numbers (odd numbers are associated with funerals)" should be grouped as a subpoint of the "*lai see*" topic because it provides more detail as to what "*lai see*" is and how it works.

Finally, "Parade floats" makes a lot more sense in the "Chinese New Year parade" paragraph than it does in the "Preparing for the Chinese New Year" paragraph. Clearly, floats are yet another feature of the parade, in addition to the firecrackers, the musical instruments, the lion dancers, and the dragon. When writing a clear, well-organized essay, it is always important to keep similar ideas together so as to maintain a logical sequence of events and descriptions. (1-point answer)

2. You should have checked the following sentences: **Lion heads are created out of papier-mâché and painted red, yellow, green, and orange.** *and* **The dragon, which symbolizes the Emperor, zig-zags down the street, breathing real fire and smoke.** These two sentences discuss key features of the parade celebration. The other two sentences belong in the paragraph that discusses how to prepare for the Chinese New Year. (1-point answer)

3. **Answers will vary. Below are sample 2-point, 1-point, and 0-point responses.**

2 Points	This response: > includes a strong topic sentence and a strong concluding sentence > includes all information from this section of the given outline > provides adequate connections and/or a progression of ideas that contribute to coherence	To celebrate the Chinese New Year, people decorate their homes in a variety of ways. Since the new year comes in spring, blooming branches of peaches, almonds, or apricots are brought indoors. Oranges, kumquats, and tangerines are arranged since sweet fruit symbolizes a "sweet life." Pears, however, are avoided since "separation" and "pear" are the same word in Chinese. Many people hang red lanterns and images of the Chinese zodiac. Messages of good luck are written in elaborate calligraphy and displayed in the home. People prepare traditional dishes of narcissus and daffodil bulbs for friends and family. Beautiful symbols of spring and good luck festoon the entire home.
1 Point	This response: > mostly follows traditional paragraph arrangement > includes most of the information from this section of the given outline > contains some parts that may be inadequate and/or illogical	People decorate their homes for the Chinese New Year. Some people use branches of peaches, almonds, or apricots. They don't use pears. Red lanterns are hung. They like to eat narcissus bulbs and oranges.

0 Points	This response: > does not follow traditional paragraph arrangement > does not include sufficient information from this section of the given outline > is inadequate and/or illogical	They put lanterns and pictures in their houses, and they like to eat daffodils and fruit. It's a symbol of a sweet life.

Section 3

1. **(A)**, **(B)**, and **(D)** Whitman uses the image of a Captain and his crew steering a ship and returning from a long voyage as a metaphor for President Lincoln finally leading troops to victory at the end of the Civil War. "People all exulting" continues with the same metaphor, explaining that people are glad the war is over. Whitman switches the metaphor from "Captain" to "father" to demonstrate the speaker's affection for President Lincoln as that of a son's affection for his father. Whitman also sometimes addresses President Lincoln directly, saying "you." (1-point answer)

2. **(B)** *Irony* is when the outcome of expected events is actually the opposite or a contrary outcome. The ship is expected to arrive at the port safely, after having had trouble at sea, but instead the bigger problem is that the Captain dies before reaching the port. It is ironic that just as he was about to reach the destination (in Lincoln's case, the goal that he was fighting for), he dies before he gets to see the end result. The other answer choices do not contain examples of irony. (1-point answer)

3. **(A)** and **(C)** Repetition is one of the most powerful devices in literature. Anything that is repeated will have a lasting effect, so a poet will usually repeat an idea if he or she wants you to consider it from multiple angles. In this poem, Whitman emphasizes the effects of the Civil War and the assassination of President Lincoln, which were shocking and severe, and he repeats these ideas so that the reader will consider them deeply. Whitman did not repeat "fallen cold and dead" to show the reader the weather; this answer choice is silly and can easily be eliminated. Whitman was an accomplished and highly skilled poet, who wrote on many subjects. Therefore, it is unlikely that he didn't know how to write about death in any other way. Eliminate choice (D) as well. (1-point answer)

4. **Answers will vary. Below are sample 2-point, 1-point, and 0-point responses.**

2 Points	This response: > correctly explains why Whitman addresses President Lincoln as "my Captain" in this poem > uses textual evidence to support the claim > uses explanation/elaboration of the claim	In his poem "O Captain! My Captain!" Walt Whitman addresses President Abraham Lincoln. Whitman refers to President Lincoln as "my Captain" because he sees Lincoln as someone who is steering his troops to victory the same way that a captain steers a ship while out at sea. In other words, the Civil War was akin to a rough time at sea, but now the boat is coming back to the port because the war has ended. However, just as the journey (the war) is about to end, the Captain dies and cannot steer the course of the last few feet of the journey. A captain is a leader of a ship's crew, the same way that a president is a leader of the country and military. This is the analogy that Whitman is trying to create. He clearly sees Lincoln as his leader and even refers to him as "dear father," which also demonstrates his loyalty to Lincoln.
1 Point	This response: > attempts to explain why Whitman addresses President Lincoln as "my Captain" in this poem > references examples from the poem to support the claim > attempts to use explanation/ elaboration of the claim	In his poem "O Captain! My Captain!" Walt Whitman addresses President Abraham Lincoln. He sees him as someone who is piloting a boat that has been at sea. He sees him as a leader of a crew.

0 Points	This response: > incorrectly or vaguely explains why Whitman addresses President Lincoln as "my Captain" in this poem > uses vague examples from the poem to support the claim or is missing examples entirely > uses incorrect or poor explanation/elaboration of the claim	Walt Whitman thinks of President Lincoln as a leader. He liked to go on boats with him.

Section 4

1. **(C)** There are two parts to understanding this question. You must determine the influence of the invention of the tractor, and you must also recognize why there was a need for wheat in World War I. The tractor helped farmers do more work faster, and it reduced the amount of labor used. World War I was an opportunity for farmers to make more money, so they wanted to plant as much as possible to make as much money as possible. The answer to this question must include both parts. Choice (C) does that. This article does not indicate that farmers were worried about having enough to eat because of World War I. Eliminate choice (A). Choice (B) discusses the influence of the tractor, but it leaves out the second part about the demand for wheat and the money-making opportunity. Choice (D) is a silly answer choice designed to catch a person not reading the text or answer choices carefully. If you were only skimming the article and the answer choices, you might have seen the key words "tractor," "wheat," and Word War I" and not looked to see if they were put together to say something true about the article. (1-point answer)

2. **(C)** A "pun" is when one word can be used in another way because it has two meanings or because it sounds like a similar word with a different meaning. In this instance, the word "root" is the pun. In this cases, root means "center," as in that roots are the center of the Great Plains ecosystem, and root also means the part of the plant that is underground. A "metaphor" describes one thing by describing another in comparison without using "like" or "as." This sentence

does not contain a metaphor. "Hyperbole" is exaggeration, but nothing is being exaggerated here. "Alliteration" is when two or more words start with the same letter consecutively; however, these sounds do not have to be back to back. This quote does not exhibit alliteration. (1-point answer)

3. **(A)** "Exorbitant" means "highly excessive," "extreme," or "outrageous." It shows that a very large number of crops died. You can rule out "unnecessary" using context clues in the rest of the paragraph. "Healthy" is a silly answer that you can immediately eliminate since the context of the sentence should show you that it doesn't make sense. "Nearby" would fit in the sentence, but if you understand the rest of the sentence and the rest of the article, "nearby" doesn't make sense either. (1-point answer)

4. **(A)** "Witness" means "to see and experience something," so you should be looking for evidence that shows what it is like to experience these dust storms. Choices (B) and (C) can easily be eliminated because these choices do not show what it is like to witness one of these storms. Choice (D) is a little more challenging in that it describes the feeling of desperation; however, this quote does not indicate that witnessing the dust storm causes desperation. Instead, choice (A) describes what you would see if you were watching one of these dust storms. (1-point answer)

5. The two words that should be followed by a comma are "**Depression**" and "**watered**." Use a pair of commas to offset an added clause in the middle of a sentence. In the second sentence, a comma is needed after "Depression." That sentence without the parenthetical clause would read, "The horrible stock market crash of 1929 left banks without money and millions of people without jobs." Inserted into that sentence is the dependent clause, "followed by the Great Depression." The pair of commas indicate where the sentence has been sliced open and the dependent clause has been inserted. In this instance, you can think of the commas as baby parentheses. You must also use a comma when joining two independent clauses. Reread the fifth sentence, and you'll see that a comma is needed after "watered." "All the wonderful rain during the previous two decades had set up the false premise that these pastures were constantly watered" and "in fact this area was actually quite arid" are both independent clauses. You can tell they are independent if you read them by themselves and they each sound like a complete sentence. A dependent clause cannot stand alone. You cannot join independent clauses or dependent clauses with just a comma; you must also use a coordinating conjunction.

Remember the acronym "FANBOYS" for the most common conjunctions (for, and, nor, but, or, yet, so). In this instance, the conjunction is "but," which requires a comma before it. (1-point answer)

6. **Answers will vary. Below are sample 2-point, 1-point, and 0-point responses.**

2 Points	This response: > correctly identifies that "Think of how annoying it is to get sand in your eyes. Now imagine all the air swirling with dirt hitting you and blackening the sky" are the sentences that need to be edited to maintain a formal style and an objective tone > replaces these sentences' casual tone with an academic tone, while maintaining pertinent information	Dust storms cause much more destruction than the simple annoyance of getting sand in one's eyes. They cause the air to swirl, blasting dirt all around and blackening the sky. There is fine dust as well as gritty dust, and it gets everywhere.
1 Point	This response: > correctly identifies that "Think of how annoying it is to get sand in your eyes. Now imagine all the air swirling with dirt hitting you and blackening the sky" are the sentences that need to be edited to maintain a formal style and an objective tone > replaces these sentences' casual tone with an academic tone, but does not maintain all pertinent information	Dust storms cause destruction. They cause the air to swirl, blasting dirt all around.

0 Points	This response:	
	> does not correctly identify that "Think of how annoying it is to get sand in your eyes. Now imagine all the air swirling with dirt hitting you and blackening the sky" are the sentences that need to be edited to maintain a formal style and an objective tone > does not replace these sentences' casual tone with an academic tone	Wow, the grating and scratching from the heavier dust is like sandpaper!

7. **Answers will vary. Below are sample 2-point, 1-point, and 0-point responses.**

2 Points	This response:	
	> gives sufficient evidence of the writer's ability to establish a claim > includes specific examples/ details that make clear reference to the text > adequately explains and supports the claim with clearly relevant information from the text	Fellow Congressmen, we must act quickly to save the farms and natural prairies of the Great Plains. Perhaps you are aware that recent droughts and over-plowing have depleted this rich land of valuable prairie grasses that hold the very earth down. As a result, the rich soil is blowing away. This might seem to you like only a setback, but the way in which the soil is blowing away is now a health crisis that requires a humanitarian response. The soil is caught up in dust storms that choke little children and adults alike. Farmers are unable to harvest their crops, which is forcing them to abandon their farms in search of another way to feed their hungry families. Just look out the window right now, and you will see the effects swirling around our city, all these hundreds of miles away. We must create some relief and regulations to help out the prairie region.

1 Point	This response: > gives limited evidence of the writer's ability to establish a claim > includes vague and/or limited examples/details that make reference to the text > explains the claim with vague and/or limited information from the text	Fellow Congressmen, we must act quickly to save the farms and natural prairies of the Great Plains. There has been a drought, and farmers have used too much soil. It is now blowing away. Farmers can't farm. Look out the window right now.
0 Points	This response: > gives no evidence of the writer's ability to establish a claim > gives a claim, but includes no examples/details that make reference to the text > gives a claim, but includes no explanation or relevant information from the text	Fellow Congressmen, we must do something. Look out the window. There is a lot of dust from farms.

Section 5

1. **Part A: (B)** This is a "central idea" question, so you should be sure to determine which choice encompasses the main idea of the essay. Choice (B) includes all "people around the world," which is essential to the central idea of this essay. The entire essay discusses the idea of celebrating a birthday in many different ways, and then concludes by suggesting that the reader should adopt a new tradition. Often, the test makers will give you answer choices that only apply to a small portion of the text, so eliminate any choices that are too narrow. This essay considers birthday traditions from all over the world, so choices (A) and (D) can quickly be eliminated since they too narrowly focus on "Germany" or "Americans and Europeans." When we consider that choice (D) only discusses birthday cakes, it becomes even narrower. Choice (C) only considers the Romans' contributions to birthday traditions, which is still too

narrow. (1-point answer, but is dependent on answering Part B correctly as well—if either Part A or Part B is answered incorrectly, the point is not awarded)

Part B: (A) and **(D)** The answer to Part A discussed "new celebrations from other cultures." A "birthday party" and "tugging on the birthday boy's or girl's ear" are specific traditions that are part of birthday celebrations. The other two answer choices are not birthday traditions. (This part is worth 0 points, but is dependent on answering Part A correctly as well—if either Part A or Part B is answered incorrectly, the point for Part A is not awarded)

2. **(B)** All of the answer choices are prepositions that make it hard to determine which is the correct answer and which are the wrong answers if you don't know the actual definition of "in lieu." There aren't a lot of tricks that you can use for a question like this. You might think it is strange that bread with sprinkles and birthday cake might be served at the same time. The three wrong choices, choices (A), (C), and (D), are all prepositions that seem to indicate that the bread with sprinkles and the birthday cake would be served together. The only answer choice where the bread with sprinkles actually replaces the birthday cake is choice (B). (1-point answer)

3. **(A)** and **(D)** Choices (A) and (D) can be inferred from this sentence. The first part of this sentence says "As far as we know." Therefore, historians do not have a lot of information about birthday celebrations for non-royal individuals prior to Roman history. Furthermore, since the author of this essay is not entirely certain that the Romans were the first culture to celebrate the birthday of someone who was not royalty, it is entirely possible that other cultures may have started this tradition. However, without concrete evidence, that claim cannot be made. Choices (B) and (C) are not facts supported by this sentence. (1-point answer)

4. **(C)** You must make an inference in regard to what is going on. You have several context clues that can help you make this inference. First, the excerpt states that the name *shou mian* means "long-life," and you know that a birthday celebration is a celebration of one's life. The excerpt also states that the birthday person should "symbolically slurp in as much of the long noodle as possible before biting." The fact that the word "symbolically" is used means that the length of the noodle likely represents something. In this case, the longer the noodle, the longer the life. This excerpt does not talk about the nutrition needed to live a long life, so choice (D) should be eliminated. Choices (A) and (B) are too general and do not exactly define what is going on in the quoted sentences. (1-point answer)

5. **(C)** There were 9 sentences that contain references to wishes or luck in total. Those references are:

   1. "By this time, making a wish and blowing out candles became a tradition."

   2. "Some people even make a wish when slicing the birthday cake."

   3. "It is considered bad luck to take a bite of cake before the birthday boy or girl takes a bite."

   4. "The 'spanking machine,' where the birthday boy or girl crawls through a lineup of friends and relatives to be playfully spanked, is similar to the United Kingdom's tradition of turning the birthday boy or girl upside down and 'bumping' him or her on the ground once for each year he or she has been alive, plus an additional bump for luck."

   5. "Scotland seems to be the origin of a popular Canadian birthday tradition about luck."

   6. "'Nose grease,' or butter, is put on the birthday boy's or girl's nose so bad luck will slip off."

   7. "In Brazil, they crack an egg on the head of the birthday person, also for luck."

   8. "A red envelope filled with money and good luck is given in both Malaysia and Vietnam."

   9. "The birthday person symbolically slurps in as much of the long noodle as possible before biting to wish for a long life."

   (1-point answer)

6. **celebrates** Reading the sentences and substituting the various choices is likely your best strategy. You will likely pick the choice that sounds right to you. This question is testing to see if you know what tense should be used. (1-point answer)

7. **(C)** Choice (D) is the easiest to eliminate since this essay does not discuss travel at all. Choice (A) should also be eliminated because this essay does not encourage the reader to throw a birthday party for other cultures. There is no discussion of throwing a party for other cultures. Rather, the essay discusses birthday traditions *from* other cultures. Choice (B) is a strong choice, but that is more of the main idea of the essay. It does not explain why the author ends the essay with these three lines of text as this question asks. The final question ("What new tradition will you adopt this year?") seems to press the reader to be

more open-minded about accepting other cultures' birthday traditions, leaving choice (C) as the only correct option. (1-point answer)

8. **Answers will vary. Below are sample 2-point, 1-point, and 0-point responses.**

| 2 Points | This response:
> focuses on personal birthday traditions
> provides appropriate and mainly specific details
> uses adequate sensory, concrete, and/or figurative language | I look forward to my birthday every year because my family creates a very special experience for me. When I wake up, my parents always give me an extra hug and make pancakes with extra syrup, which is my favorite breakfast. Then I usually have to go to school because my birthday is on April 20. When I was little, my parents used to pretend the "Birthday Bear" would leave presents for me. As I have gotten older, we no longer practice that tradition, but we do continue the tradition of "birthday power." This means that if there are any family decisions to be made that day, I get to have the final say. For instance, when we are thinking of what to do for dinner, I always opt for pizza at a local restaurant in town because pizza is my favorite dinner. We then come home, open presents, and eat the homemade cake my mom makes from the lemons exploding off the tree in our backyard. My favorite tradition, however, is reading what my family writes on the birthday cards they give me. They are always full of favorite memories of the year and special wishes. I keep a box with all of these cards. |

1 Point	This response: > vaguely discusses personal birthday traditions > provides mostly general descriptive details and may include extraneous details that are unrelated or only loosely related > uses limited sensory, concrete, and/or figurative language	I look forward to my birthday every year. My parents make me pancakes. Then I usually have to go to school because my birthday is on April 20. I like to eat pizza, lemon cake, and open presents.
0 Points	This response: > does not discuss personal birthday traditions > includes few, if any, descriptive details that may be vague, repetitive, or incorrect and/or those details may interfere with the meaning of the narrative > uses little or no sensory, concrete, and/or figurative language	My parents make me pancakes. Then I eat pizza and cake.

Section 6

1. **The correct numbers are listed below.**

   (4) Zitkala-Sa and her friends search for little crystal drops of gum.

   (5) Zitkala-Sa and her friends pretend to trade personal items.

   (1) Mother begins her beadwork after breakfast.

   (6) Zitkala-Sa and her friends pretend to be their mothers.

   (9) Zitkala-Sa and her friends return one another's borrowed items and go home.

   (3) Zitkala-Sa and her friends search for sweet roots, which they harvest with rods.

   (7) Zitkala-Sa and her friends tell exciting stories.

   (8) Zitkala-Sa tries to catch her shadow.

   (2) Zitkala-Sa observes her mother's designs for her daughter's moccasins.

You should approach this task in two stages. First, try to arrange the sentences in order based on your memory of the story and any logic you can apply to the sequence of events. Then check your arrangement with the text itself, by skimming and rereading. This task is straightforward, but in another task, you may need to skim and reread the original text more closely to determine exactly what happened in what order. (1-point answer)

2. **Part A: (A)** The sentence "With a proud, beaming face, I watched her work" would seem to indicate that Zitkala-Sa is proud of her mother and likes her mother's work. The rest of the second paragraph discusses the details of her mother's process. The next four paragraphs after that discuss Zitkala-Sa's own practice. She may be slightly "intimidated" by her mother's skill, but it certainly does not make her angry, so choice (B) is incorrect. Choices (C) and (D) are not supported by the text. (1-point answer, but is dependent on answering Part B correctly as well—if either Part A or Part B is answered incorrectly, the point is not awarded)

    Part B: (B) and **(D)** These two choices support the idea that Zitkala-Sa is in awe of her mother's skill. Clearly, the mother's skill made Zitkala-Sa proud. Furthermore, the mother's "quietness of her oversight," shows that the mother is a good teacher to her daughter whose teaching encourages her daughter to trust her own judgment when working on her own beading. Choice (A) does not discuss Zitkala-Sa's feelings towards her mother. Choice (C) discusses the logistics of the work itself, but it does not discuss how Zitkala-Sa feels about her mother or her mother's skill. (This part is worth 0 points, but is dependent on answering Part A correctly as well—if either Part A or Part B is answered incorrectly, the point for Part A is not awarded)

3. **(B)** and **(C)** Choice (B) shows the children pretending to act like adults but mimicking the things they've seen and heard from their parents. Choice (C) shows the narrator, a child, trying to step on her shadow, an act that only a child would think is possible. The other two choices are much more literal and descriptive, discussing the beadwork process. (1-point answer)

Section 7

1. **Answers will vary. A sample response is provided below.**

    A sweaty woman wearing a black miniskirt and a white blouse rushed into the lobby. Her red hair partially hid an old scar on her forehead. As she glanced around, her floral perfume trailed her. The old-fashioned black doctor's bag pulled her shoulder downward and tugged at her blouse. She turned her kind eyes to me and asked worriedly, "Where is room 1120?" I said, "Eleventh floor—to your left." Just then the elevator doors dinged open, and a man clutching his heart fell out into the lobby.

Many details were added to enhance the narrative's sensory descriptions, using words like, "sweaty," "black miniskirt," "floral," "old-fashioned," and "dinged." These words utilize many of the five senses. Additionally, many sentences were combined to help the description flow more smoothly. To create more excitement, many of the verbs were switched from weak or general verbs to more precise and active verbs: "entered" was switched to "rushed," and "carrying" was switched to "pulled … downward … tugged." An additional description of a man clutching his heart while falling out of the elevator, paired with the detail of the doctor's bag, adds interest and suspense, thereby creating excitement. (1-point answer)

2. **Answers will vary. Below are sample 2-point, 1-point, and 0-point responses.**

| 2 Points | This response:
> focuses on the narrator's experience
> provides appropriate and mainly specific details
> uses adequate sensory, concrete, and/or figurative language | Monday, July 10 started like any other warm, summer day. I woke up at 6:30 A.M., ate scrambled eggs, and took the number 10 bus to the Grand Palace hotel, where I work as a hotel receptionist. The regular flow of guests checking out or requesting hotel services, like housekeeping or dry cleaning, created a cluster of voices, punctuated by the ding of the elevator doors. I helped seven guests with directions to the beekeeper's convention three blocks away. The constant motion of people moving reminded me of watching a room of ballroom dancers. I felt the energy in the room increasing, and I could just tell that things were about to intensify. |

1 Point	This response: > vaguely discusses the narrator's experience > provides mostly general descriptive details and may include extraneous details that are unrelated or only loosely related > uses limited sensory, concrete, and/or figurative language	It started like any other day. I woke up and took the bus to where I work as a hotel receptionist. Guests were checking out. Several guests asked me for directions to the convention in town. Another hotel was also busy.
0 Points	This response: > does not discuss the narrator's experience > includes few, if any, descriptive details that may be vague, repetitive, or incorrect; these details may interfere with the meaning of the narrative > uses little or no sensory, concrete, and/or figurative language	Guests were all around. Several guests asked for directions. Another hotel was also busy. That hotel had a pool.

Section 8

1. **(A)** and **(B)** When you read this persuasive essay, you may have noticed a jolt from "In areas where there are a lot of gangs, the school uniforms prevent students from displaying gang colors" and "People often try to steal one another's high-priced fashion items." This is because the author seems to switch subjects quite suddenly and without a transition. There are a number of ways to fix this. For instance, the author could add an additional sentence between them, like "Allowing students to show off their own clothes could also lead to other criminal behaviors." The author could also edit the second sentence and add a transition like, "Without school uniforms, students may also feel unsafe because people often try to steal one another's high-priced fashion

items." Furthermore, this paragraph is making some strong claims about violence and safety, but it doesn't have any real evidence to support these claims. Including additional evidence that shows that a lack of uniforms led to dangerous behaviors at not just one but several schools would strengthen the credibility of this argument. Other evidence could include crime statistics in several schools, or students' testimonies about their personal experiences. If the author were to begin a discussion about which colors belong to which gangs, the discussion would go off topic, so eliminate choice (C). Similarly, "national crime statistics" are not going to be helpful to this argument because those numbers will include all sorts of crimes, not just those that may happen in schools due to the dress code. Therefore, choice (D) is incorrect as well. (1-point answer)

2. **(D)** The nice thing about these answer choices is that they are like a recipe for how to build a paragraph. "Many schools have adopted school uniforms to create a more level playing field for poor students" is the topic sentence, so eliminate choice (A). "Often fashion trends are influenced by heavy marketing, whose target is to get students to buy expensive clothing and shoes" and "About 50 percent of cities where lower-class students go to school require uniforms, and that number is rising. Ninety-five percent of New Orleans students wear uniforms to school every day because 39 percent of their children live below the poverty line, which is 17 points higher than the national average" are all supportive evidence. They even include concrete facts and data that have been researched. "This puts unnecessary pressure on some lower-income families who can't afford to keep up with the trends. Being fashionable has absolutely no place in obtaining an education. More and more schools agree with that statement" and "School uniforms are helping New Orleans parents make sending their kids to school a bit more affordable" are all adequate explanations of the supportive evidence and great commentaries on that evidence. What is missing is a concluding sentence, which should be like a bookend to the topic sentence about how school uniforms help combat classism. The current last sentence in the paragraph may seem like a concluding sentence, but it only discusses the situation in New Orleans whereas the topic sentence more generally talks about combatting classism in all schools. (1-point answer)

3. The sentence that should be edited to be more formal in tone is: **"It also discourages the idea of any one person being a superstar or a loser."** The words "superstar" and "loser" are very casual. Possible replacements for

"superstar" might be "elite" or "popular." Possible replacements for "loser" might be "outcast" or "unpopular." (1-point answer)

4. **Part A: (B)** Choices (A) and (B) are pulled from the first paragraph, which is where the claim is usually stated. Like other tasks that ask you to find the main or general idea, the claim has to be broad enough to fit with the entire text. Between choices (A) and (B), ask yourself which of these statements best applies to the whole text. Choice (A) discusses possible uniforms. Choice (B) discusses improving student learning and increasing school safety. That is clearly the argument that the author used throughout this persuasive essay, so choice (B) is the correct answer. Choice (C) comes from the conclusion paragraph and is concluding in nature, but it does not address the two themes of the essay: improving student learning and increasing school safety. Choice (D) is a topic sentence that addresses combatting classism. (1-point answer, but is dependent on answering Part B correctly as well—if either Part A or Part B is answered incorrectly, the point is not awarded)

Part B: (C) and **(D)** Choices (C) and (D) support the claim that uniforms improve student learning and increase school safety. Choices (A) and (B) both discuss the counterargument that school uniforms stifle free choice and self-expression, but they do not support the claim that school uniforms improve student learning and increase school safety. (This part is worth 0 points, but is dependent on answering Part A correctly as well—if either Part A or Part B is answered incorrectly, the point for Part A is not awarded)

5. **Answers will vary. Below are sample 2-point, 1-point, and 0-point responses.**

| 2 Points | This response:
> clearly identifies the correct counterargument
> cites textual evidence from the essay for that counterargument
> explains/elaborates on the counterargument | The author of "School Uniforms Help Students" supports wearing school uniforms and refutes the counterargument that "self-expression suffers [when students wear uniforms] and that free choice allows students to experiment with who they are and who they might become." This counterargument suggests that students have a need to express who they are and that they need freedom of fashion expression to develop properly as human beings. The author refutes this argument by suggesting that there are other opportunities for students to express themselves. |

For instance, students can wear whatever they want "after school or on the weekends." Furthermore, the author makes the great point that "students are more likely to copy one another, following trends, than to branch out and develop a sense of self." Therefore, when given the choice to dress themselves, students will most likely just copy the popular trends than choose something that represents themselves. The author also suggests that opportunities to accessorize might also be available for the purpose of self-expression and then the author returns to the claim that school uniforms help students focus in school and decrease safety concerns.

1 Point	This response: > somewhat identifies the correct counterargument > references examples from the essay for that counterargument > attempts to explain/elaborate on the counterargument	The author of "School Uniforms Help Students" supports wearing school uniforms and argues against the idea that students need to wear their own choice of clothes. This idea means that students have to use clothes to express who they are, but the author disagrees with this idea.
0 Points	This response: > does not identify the correct counterargument > presents either vague examples from the essay for that counterargument or does not provide any examples at all > incorrectly or poorly explains/elaborates on the counterargument.	The author of "School Uniforms Help Students" thinks that wearing your own clothes is bad because you are just copying your friends, like if they have the same shoes, then you also want them.

Performance Task (pages 135–148)

Part 1

1. **Answers will vary. Below are sample 2-point, 1-point, and 0-point responses.**

2 Points	This response: > clearly demonstrates an understanding of the prompt > demonstrates an understanding of the stimulus text > uses details from the stimulus text	The process of manufacturing steel was dangerous to steelworkers for a variety of reasons. According to John Stone, in his article entitled "A Brief History of the U.S. Steelmaking Industry," the molten iron "could cause severe and deadly burns" to workers. Even when cooled, the steel was heavy and could easily crush a steelworker in addition to creating "crippling back and skeletal injuries" as Stone points out. Additionally, constant coal dust floating in the air entered the workers' lungs, creating a lifelong disease called "black lung." Poor working conditions in steel mills also created additional dangers, such as workers falling from tall heights or "having hot metal splinters fly into their eyes." The loud work also had the potential to cause "permanent hearing loss." The risks for danger were significantly increased by the lack of training and safety regulations in the steel manufacturing industry during its early days.
1 Point	This response: > demonstrates some understanding of the prompt and the stimulus text > uses vague references to the stimulus text	The process of manufacturing steel was dangerous to steelworkers for a variety of reasons. They could get burned and/or crushed by the steel. Coal dust could make them sick too. People fell sometimes. They got poked in the eye, and it was too loud in the steel mills.
0 Points	This response: > does not demonstrate an understanding of the prompt and the stimulus text > does not refer to any part of the stimulus text	People got burned and fell. It was loud.

2. **Answers will vary. Below are sample 2-point, 1-point, and 0-point responses.**

2 Points	This response: > clearly demonstrates an understanding of the prompt > demonstrates an understanding of the stimulus text > uses details from the stimulus text	Through many years of struggles, the steelworkers' unions helped improve the lives and working conditions of the steelworkers. After the Wagner Act was passed in Congress in 1935, unions were legally allowed to form and fight for their members ("United States Steel Labor Unions"). As a result of several steel strikes, and the formation of the Steel Workers Organizing Committee, wages eventually increased and long shifts were reduced to more reasonable hours. The Occupational Safety and Health Act, passed in Congress in 1970, made "employers responsible for safe working conditions" ("United States Steel Labor Unions"). It is very unlikely any of these improved working conditions would have happened without the hard fights fought by these unions.
1 Point	This response: > demonstrates some understanding of the prompt and the stimulus text > uses vague references to the stimulus text	The steelworkers' unions helped improve the lives and working conditions of the steelworkers. These improvements included better wages, shorter shifts, and safer conditions.
0 Points	This response: > does not demonstrate an understanding of the prompt and the stimulus text > does not refer to any part of the stimulus text	The steelworkers' unions were able to get improvements from the employers.

3. **Answers will vary. Below are sample 2-point, 1-point, and 0-point responses.**

2 Points	This response: > clearly demonstrates an understanding of the prompt > demonstrates an understanding of the stimulus text > uses details from the stimulus text	According to the article "United States Steel Labor Unions," posted on SteelLaborHistory.com, a labor union is "an organization of workers who band together to protect workers' interests." These united workers fight for "safer working conditions, fair wages, or reasonable working hours." Unions are necessary because sometimes employers do not pay their workers a fair amount or they overwork their employees. Employers might even neglect to provide safe working conditions, making the workplace dangerous. This is where unions step in to fight for better treatment. Once organized, the union elects a leader who shares the workers' concerns with the employer. If the employer does not address these concerns, the workers can band together and strike, which hurts the companies. Striking is often a last resort for workers because stepping away from their jobs to protest hurts those workers who "need their jobs to provide for their families." By teaming up together, however, the workers are a stronger unit than if they were to each protest individually. For many, the chance to see change happen is worth the risk.
1 Point	This response: > demonstrates some understanding of the prompt and the stimulus text > uses vague references to the stimulus text	A labor union helps workers when their employers are being unfair. They strike. Sometimes this makes employers lose business and give in, but sometimes the employer fights back.

0 Points	This response:	Employers can be unfair, so unions elect leaders.
	> does not demonstrate an understanding of the prompt and the stimulus text	
	> does not refer to any part of the stimulus text	

Part 2

Answers will vary. Below are sample criteria for 4-point, 3-point, 2-point, and 1-point responses.

Explanatory Score: 4	
Organization/Purpose	This response has a clear and effective organizational structure that creates a sense of unity and completeness. The organization is fully sustained between and within paragraphs. This response is consistently and purposefully focused. > The thesis/controlling idea of the topic is clearly communicated, and the focus is strongly maintained for the purpose and audience. > There is consistent use of a variety of transitional strategies to clarify the relationships between and among ideas. There is also an effective introduction and conclusion. > There is a logical progression of ideas from beginning to end. There are strong connections between and among ideas with some syntactic variety.
Evidence/Elaboration	This response provides adequate elaboration of the support/evidence for the thesis/controlling ideas that include the use of source material. This response adequately develops ideas, employing a mix of precise and more general language. > Comprehensive evidence (facts and details) from the source material is integrated, relevant, and specific. > There are clear citations or attributions to the source material.

Evidence/Elaboration (continued)	> There is effective use of a variety of elaborative techniques (which may include the use of personal experiences that support the controlling idea). > The vocabulary is clearly appropriate for the audience and purpose. > An effective, appropriate style enhances the content.

Conventions Score: 2

This response demonstrates an adequate command of conventions and an adequate use of correct sentence formation, punctuation, capitalization, grammar usage, and spelling.

Most workers in America enjoy safe working conditions and an 8-hour workday. This wasn't true over 130 years ago. Going to work might mean going to your grave. As a result of the Industrial Revolution, more people were living in cities and working in manufacturing jobs, like textile mills and steel mills. Many people were killed or injured, especially because they were working such long hours. They weren't even paid very well. The workers often tried to ask for more money and better working conditions, but the employers didn't want to make changes. Many workers started rebelling, realizing that they could band together and refuse to work, which would hurt the employers financially. However, this also meant that the striking workers wouldn't get paid and risked being fired. It was a risk that paid off slowly. Over the years, the laborers formed unions and fought for better working conditions and pay. The steelworkers were one of the groups that fought the hardest for their rights, most likely because their jobs were some of the most dangerous types of employment.

In 1931, artist John Kane created a romantic portrayal of the steel industry in his painting, "The Monongahela River Valley, Pennsylvania." In this painting, you can see smoke rising from the many factories as trains come in and out, loaded with materials for trade. This image depicts only part of what it was like in early America with the rise of steel mill factories and the effect they had on American society ("The Monongahela River Valley, Pennsylvania"). Being a steelworker was not at all as romantic and picturesque as the painting might make it seem. Being a steelworker was actually very treacherous. Melting the steel meant working with a lot of heat. Working in the furnace required workers to be around poisonous dust particles and exploding gases. Over time, steelworkers could develop "black lung" disease. Working with the metal could also expose a worker to very serious burns or to hot metal splinters ("A Brief History of the U.S. Steelmaking Industry").

Workers could be injured at any time. It was very hard work, as Langston Hughes described in his poem, "Steel Mills." He observes "The Mills / that grind and grind, / that grind out steel / and grind away lives / of men." He describes how these men literally worked their lives away with the monotonous motion of grinding day after day. The hours were long, too. It was often the case that "most people worked six days a week," and they often worked "sometimes as long as 12 hours" a day ("A Brief History of the U.S. Steelmaking Industry"). Even children were employed to do dangerous work. Sometimes everyone in the family worked to try to make a living because the pay was so terrible. Workers, especially immigrants, did not get enough training. As a result, "each year, about 25 percent of the immigrant workers were killed or injured on the job, which was double that of white Americans" ("A Brief History of the U.S. Steelmaking Industry"). Workers were literally dying, so something had to be done. The answer was for the steelworkers to go on strike.

At first, the steel strikes didn't go so well. The steel mills were very aggressive and even physically attacked the strikers. Some of the "early strikes were often met with angry actions from employers, who would hire security guards or temporary workers, called 'scabs'" and "employers' security would fire into crowds or set off tear gas to disperse the protesters" ("United States Steel Labor Unions"). It didn't seem like striking was going to help the workers. It hurt the employers financially, but it hurt the employees financially, too, because they weren't getting paid. Workers had an important question to ask themselves: Was it more dangerous to die at work due to unsafe working conditions, or was it more dangerous to strike and risk being shot by their bosses? Sometimes the strikes didn't last, and the workers didn't improve anything. Over time, however, as the workers kept fighting, they did improve working conditions. The workers formed unions, which gave the workers more power because the unions included employees from the other steel companies, too. The workers in these labor unions weren't just fighting their employers; they were fighting to pass laws regulating working conditions in Congress, too. In 1910, steel workers and other laborers lobbied Congress to pass the Accident Reports Act, which created the ten-hour workday ("United States Steel Labor Unions"). This new law was a big improvement for the overworked employees. Since workers would no longer be so sleepy, they wouldn't have as many accidents. Battle by battle, and sometimes by gun battle, the workers fought successfully to increase their wages and to improve their working conditions. They even ended child labor. Perhaps their greatest achievement was in 1970 when "Congress passed the Occupational

Safety and Health Act (OSHA), which made companies more responsible for worker safety. This act drastically helped improve working conditions" ("A Brief History of the U.S. Steelmaking Industry").

There is a downside to these advances, however. The steel industry suffered severely because of strikes. In 1959, the steel industry had been reporting high profits, and so, as a result, 500,000 steelworkers went on strike to try to increase their wages ("United States Steel Labor Unions"). As the years went on and as these strikes continued, companies like those in the automobile manufacturing industry "could not wait for the workers and companies to resolve disputes, so they made contracts with foreign companies and imported the steel, which crippled the U.S. steel industry" ("A Brief History of the U.S. Steelmaking Industry"). Foreign steel mills were improving their techniques and were able to make steel cheaper. Therefore, companies did not go back to U.S. steel mills for their future supplies. Even today, cheaper foreign labor puts the U.S. steel mills in a tight spot. U.S. steelworkers want more money, but their employers don't have record profits anymore.

So much has changed for workers in the last 130 or so years, fortunately for the better for the most part. The U.S. steel unions were essential in the fight for increasing wages and making working conditions livable. Workers' lives have been saved in many industries, not just the steel industry. These striking workers' actions helped pass laws that protect all workers today.

Explanatory Score: 3	
Organization/Purpose	This response has an evident organizational structure and a sense of completeness. Though there may be minor flaws, they do not interfere with the overall coherence. The organization is adequately sustained between and within paragraphs. The response is generally focused. > The thesis/controlling idea of the topic is clear, and the focus is mostly maintained for the purpose and audience. > There is an adequate use of transitional strategies with some variety to clarify the relationships between and among ideas. There is also an adequate introduction and conclusion. > There is an adequate progression of ideas from beginning to end. There are adequate connections between and among ideas.

Explanatory Score: 3	
Evidence/Elaboration	This response provides adequate elaboration of the support/evidence for the thesis/controlling ideas that include the use of source material. This response adequately develops ideas, employing a mix of precise and more general language.
	> Adequate evidence (facts and details) from the source material is integrated and relevant, yet may be general.
	> There is an adequate use of citations or attributions to the source material.
	> There is an adequate use of some elaborative techniques (which may include the use of personal experiences that support the controlling idea).
	> The vocabulary is somewhat appropriate for the audience and purpose.
	> A generally appropriate style is evident.

Conventions Score: 2
This response demonstrates an adequate command of conventions and an adequate use of correct sentence formation, punctuation, capitalization, grammar usage, and spelling.

Most workers in America enjoy safe working conditions and an 8-hour workday. This wasn't true over 130 years ago. Going to work might mean going to your grave. Many people were killed or injured, especially because they were working such long hours and for what? They weren't paid very well. They tried to ask for more money and better working conditions, but the employers didn't want to make changes. Workers started rebelling by forming unions, which fought for better working conditions and pay. The steelworkers were one of the groups that fought the hardest.

Being a steelworker is dangerous. There is a lot of heat, poisonous dust, and exploding gases. Steelworkers can get "black lung" disease. They could also get burned. They worked "six days a week" and "sometimes as long as 12 hours" a day ("A Brief History of the U.S. Steelmaking Industry"). The pay was terrible. People were literally dying, so something had to be done. The steelworkers went on strike.

At first, the steel strikes didn't go so well. The steel mills were very aggressive and even would fire into crowds or set off tear gas. There were gun fights too! The strikes didn't work well at first, but over time they helped improve working conditions. The workers formed unions, which made them more powerful. The unions also talked to Congress to get laws passed. In 1910, Congress passed the Accident Reports Act, which created the ten-hour workday ("United States Steel Labor Unions"). Over time, the unions increased the workers' wages and improved their working conditions. In 1970, "Congress passed the Occupational Safety and Health Act (OSHA), which made companies more responsible for worker safety" ("A Brief History of the U.S. Steelmaking Industry").

So much has changed for workers in the last 130 or so years, fortunately for the better. The U.S. steel unions were essential in the fight for increasing wages and making working conditions livable. Workers' lives have been saved and in more than just the steel industry. Their actions have helped pass laws that protect all workers.

Explanatory Score: 2	
Organization/Purpose	This response has an inconsistent organizational structure. Some flaws are evident, and some ideas may be loosely connected. The organization is somewhat sustained between and within paragraphs. This response may have a minor drift in focus.
	> The thesis/controlling idea of the topic may be somewhat unclear, or the focus may be insufficiently maintained for the purpose and/or audience.
	> There is an inconsistent use of transitional strategies and/or little variety. The introduction or conclusion, if present, may be weak.
	> There is an uneven progression of ideas from beginning to end, and/or these ideas may be formulaic. There are inconsistent or unclear connections between and among ideas.

Explanatory Score: 2	
Evidence/Elaboration	This response provides an uneven, cursory elaboration of the support/evidence for the thesis/controlling ideas that include the uneven or limited use of source material. This response develops ideas unevenly, using simplistic language.
	> Some evidence (facts and details) from the source material may be weakly integrated, imprecise, repetitive, vague, and/or copied.
	> There is weak use of citations or attributions to the source material.
	> There is weak or uneven use of elaborative techniques (which may include personal experiences that support the controlling idea). These techniques may consist primarily of source summary.
	> The vocabulary is not entirely appropriate for the audience and purpose.
	> The style is not entirely appropriate.
Conventions Score: 1	

This response demonstrates a partial command of conventions and a limited use of correct sentence formation, punctuation, capitalization, grammar usage, and spelling.

Lots of steelworkers were hurt and not paid well so they made unions that could help them get more money and not have to complete dangerous work.

There are a lot of dangerous things for steelworkers. Breathing in that dust has created a lifelong disease, called "black lung", which doctors mistakenly thought was tuberculous at first. Coal dust is not the only deadly thing to breathe in; carbon monoxide and other hot gases are dangerous for workers' lungs. Even more frightening, those gases sometimes explode. They could also get burned. They pay was terrible. The steelworkers went on strike. The bosses attacked the strikers with gun fights! Then they got more powerful. They got more money and pay. Now there are not as many dangers at work.

The workers fought real hard for their money!

Explanatory Score: 1	
Organization/Purpose	This response has little or no discernible organizational structure. This response may be related to the topic, but it may demonstrate little or no focus. > The thesis/controlling idea of the topic may be confusing or ambiguous. This response may be too brief, or the focus may drift from the purpose and/or audience. > Few transitional strategies are evident, or there are none at all. The introduction and/or conclusion may be missing. > Frequent extraneous ideas may be evident. Ideas may be randomly ordered or have an unclear progression.
Evidence/Elaboration	This response provides minimal elaboration of the support/evidence for the thesis/controlling ideas that include little or no use of the source material. This response is vague, lacks clarity, or is confusing. > Evidence (facts and details) from the source material is minimal, irrelevant, absent, incorrectly used, or predominantly copied. > There is an insufficient use of citations or attributions to the source material. > There is minimal, if any, use of elaborative techniques (which may include the use of personal experiences that support the controlling idea). > The vocabulary is limited or ineffective for the audience and purpose. > There is little or no evidence of appropriate style.
Conventions Score: 0	
This response demonstrates little or no command of conventions and an infrequent use of correct sentence formation, punctuation, capitalization, grammar usage, and spelling.	

Lots of workers were hurt and not payed well so they made unions that could help them get more money. They could also get burned. There money was terrible. The workers striked. They got shot, then they had gun fights, then they got more money and pay. Now there is no danger at work. They fought real hard for more money.

How to Use the Smarter Balanced Performance Task Scoring Rubrics

When the SBAC scores your writing, there are certain skills and elements that they look for. A rubric organizes these elements by level of mastery. Each level of mastery is given a score. It is helpful for you to understand these different levels so you can write with these expectations in mind. Actually, it is encouraged to treat the rubrics as a checklist. When you are done with your writing, check it against each element in the rubric.

Smarter Balanced Performance Task Scoring Rubrics

4-Point Argumentative Performance Task Rubric (Grades 6–11)	
Score	Organization/Purpose
4	The response has a clear and effective organizational structure, creating a sense of unity and completeness. The organization is fully sustained between and within paragraphs. The response is consistently and purposefully focused: > claim is introduced, clearly communicated, and the focus is strongly maintained for the purpose and audience > consistent use of a variety of transitional strategies to clarify the relationships between and among ideas > effective introduction and conclusion > logical progression of ideas from beginning to end; strong connections between and among ideas with some syntactic variety > alternate and opposing argument(s) are clearly acknowledged or addressed*

3	The response has an evident organizational structure and a sense of completeness. Though there may be minor flaws, they do not interfere with the overall coherence. The organization is adequately sustained between and within the paragraphs. The response is generally focused:
	> claim is clear, and the focus is mostly maintained for the purpose and audience
	> adequate use of transitional strategies with some variety to clarify relationships between and among ideas
	> adequate introduction and conclusion
	> adequate progression of ideas from beginning to end; adequate connections between and among ideas
	> alternate and opposing argument(s) are adequately acknowledged or addressed*
2	The response has an inconsistent organizational structure. Some flaws are evident and some ideas may be loosely connected. The organization is somewhat sustained between and within paragraphs. The response may have a minor drift in focus:
	> claim may be somewhat unclear, or the focus may be insufficiently sustained for the purpose and/or audience
	> inconsistent use of transitional strategies and/or little variety
	> introduction or conclusion, if present, may be weak
	> uneven progression of ideas from beginning to end; and/or formulaic; inconsistent or unclear connections among ideas
	> alternate and opposing argument(s) may be confusing or not acknowledged*
1	The response has little or no discernible organizational structure. The response may be related to the claim but may provide little or no focus:
	> claim may be confusing or ambiguous; response may be too brief or the focus may drift from the purpose and/or audience
	> few or no transitional strategies are evident
	> introduction and/or conclusion may be missing
	> frequent extraneous ideas may be evident; ideas may be randomly ordered or have unclear progression
	> alternate and opposing argument(s) may not be acknowledged*

NS	> Insufficient (includes copied text)
	> In a language other than English
	> Off-topic
	> Off-purpose

*Acknowledging and/or addressing the opposing point of view begins at grade 7.

Score	Evidence/Elaboration
4	The response provides thorough and convincing elaboration of the support/evidence for the claim and argument(s) including reasoned, in-depth analysis and the effective use of source material. The response clearly and effectively develops ideas using precise language: > comprehensive evidence (facts and details) from the source material is integrated, relevant, and specific > clear citations or attribution to source material > effective use of a variety of elaborative techniques* > vocabulary is clearly appropriate for the audience and purpose > effective, appropriate style enhances content
3	The response provides adequate elaboration of the support/ evidence for the claim and argument(s) that includes reasoned analysis and the use of source material. The response adequately develops ideas, employing a mix of precise with more general language: > adequate evidence (facts and details) from the source material is integrated and relevant, yet may be general > adequate use of citations or attribution to source material > adequate use of some elaborative techniques* > vocabulary is generally appropriate for the audience and purpose > generally appropriate style is evident

2	The response provides uneven, cursory elaboration of the support/ evidence for the claim and argument(s) that includes some reasoned analysis and partial or uneven use of source material. The response develops ideas unevenly, using simplistic language: > some evidence (facts and details) from the source material may be weakly integrated, imprecise, repetitive, vague, and/or copied > weak use of citations or attribution to source material > weak or uneven use of elaborative techniques*; development may consist primarily of source summary or may rely on emotional appeal > vocabulary use is uneven or somewhat ineffective for the audience and purpose > inconsistent or weak attempt to create appropriate style
1	The response provides minimal elaboration of the support/evidence for the claim and argument(s) that includes little or no use of source material. The response is vague, lacks clarity, or is confusing: > evidence (facts and details) from the source material is minimal, irrelevant, absent, incorrectly used, or predominantly copied > insufficient use of citations or attribution to source material > minimal, if any, use of elaborative techniques*; emotional appeal may dominate > vocabulary is limited or ineffective for the audience and purpose > little or no evidence of appropriate style
NS	> Insufficient (includes copied text) > In a language other than English > Off-topic > Off-purpose

*Elaborative techniques may include the use of personal experiences that support the argument(s).

	2-Point Argumentative Performance Task Writing Rubric (Grades 6–11)
Score	**Conventions**
2	**The response demonstrates an adequate command of conventions:** › adequate use of correct sentence formation, punctuation, capitalization, grammar usage, and spelling
1	**The response demonstrates a partial command of conventions:** › limited use of correct sentence formation, punctuation, capitalization, grammar usage, and spelling
0	**The response demonstrates little or no command of conventions:** › infrequent use of correct sentence formation, punctuation, capitalization, grammar usage, and spelling
NS	› Insufficient (includes copied text) › In a language other than English › Off-topic › Off-purpose

Holistic Scoring:
› **Variety:** A range of errors includes sentence formation, punctuation, capitalization, grammar usage, and spelling.
› **Severity:** Basic errors are more heavily weighted than higher-level errors.
› **Density:** The proportion of errors to the amount of writing done well. This includes the ratio of errors to the length of the piece.

	4-Point Explanatory Performance Task Writing Rubric (Grades 6–11)
Score	**Organization/Purpose**
4	The response has a clear and effective organizational structure, creating a sense of unity and completeness. The organization is fully sustained between and within paragraphs. The response is consistently and purposefully focused: > thesis/controlling idea of a topic is clearly communicated, and the focus is strongly maintained for the purpose and audience > consistent use of a variety of transitional strategies to clarify the relationships between and among ideas > effective introduction and conclusion > logical progression of ideas from beginning to end; strong connections between and among ideas with some syntactic variety
3	The response has an evident organizational structure and a sense of completeness. Though there may be minor flaws, they do not interfere with the overall coherence. The organization is adequately sustained between and within paragraphs. The response is generally focused: > thesis/controlling idea of a topic is clear, and the focus is mostly maintained for the purpose and audience > adequate use of transitional strategies with some variety to clarify the relationships between and among ideas > adequate introduction and conclusion > adequate progression of ideas from beginning to end; adequate connections between and among ideas
2	The response has an inconsistent organizational structure. Some flaws are evident, and some ideas may be loosely connected. The organization is somewhat sustained between and within paragraphs. The response may have a minor drift in focus: > thesis/controlling idea of a topic may be somewhat unclear, or the focus may be insufficiently sustained for the purpose and/or audience > inconsistent use of transitional strategies and/or little variety > introduction or conclusion, if present, may be weak > uneven progression of ideas from beginning to end; and/or formulaic; inconsistent or unclear connections between and among ideas

1	The response has little or no discernible organizational structure. The response may be related to the topic but may provide little or no focus: > thesis/controlling idea may be confusing or ambiguous; response may be too brief or the focus may drift from the purpose and/or audience > few or no transitional strategies are evident > introduction and/or conclusion may be missing > frequent extraneous ideas may be evident; ideas may be randomly ordered or have an unclear progression
NS	> Insufficient (includes copied text) > In a language other than English > Off-topic > Off-purpose

Score	Evidence/Elaboration
4	The response provides thorough elaboration of the support/evidence for the thesis/controlling idea that includes the effective use of source material. The response clearly and effectively develops ideas, using precise language: > comprehensive evidence (facts and details) from the source material is integrated, relevant, and specific > clear citations or attribution to source material > effective use of a variety of elaborative techniques* > vocabulary is clearly appropriate for the audience and purpose > effective, appropriate style enhances content
3	The response provides adequate elaboration of the support/evidence for the thesis/controlling idea that includes the use of source material. The response adequately develops ideas, employing a mix of precise and more general language: > adequate evidence (facts and details) from the source material is integrated and relevant, yet may be general > adequate use of citations or attribution to source material > adequate use of elaborative techniques* > vocabulary is generally appropriate for the audience and purpose > generally appropriate style is evident

2	The response provides uneven, cursory elaboration of the support/evidence for the thesis/controlling idea that includes uneven or limited use of source material. The response develops ideas unevenly, using simplistic language: > some evidence (facts and details) from the source material may be weakly integrated, imprecise, repetitive, vague, and/or copied > weak use of citations or attribution to source material > weak or uneven use of elaborative techniques*; development may consist primarily of source summary > vocabulary use is uneven or somewhat ineffective for the audience and purpose > inconsistent or weak attempt to create appropriate style
1	The response provides minimal elaboration of the support/evidence for the thesis/controlling idea that includes little or no use of source material. The response is vague, lacks clarity, or is confusing: > evidence (facts and details) from the source material is minimal, irrelevant, absent, incorrectly used, or predominantly copied > insufficient use of citations or attribution to source material > minimal, if any, use of elaborative techniques* > vocabulary is limited or ineffective for the audience and purpose > little or no evidence of appropriate style
NS	> Insufficient (includes copied text) > In a language other than English > Off-topic > Off-purpose

*Elaborative techniques may include the use of personal experiences that support the controlling idea.

Score	2-Point Explanatory Performance Task Writing Rubric (Grades 6–11)
	Conventions
2	**The response demonstrates an adequate command of conventions:** > adequate use of correct sentence formation, punctuation, capitalization, grammar usage, and spelling
1	**The response demonstrates a partial command of conventions:** > limited use of correct sentence formation, punctuation, capitalization, grammar usage, and spelling
0	**The response demonstrates little or no command of conventions:** > infrequent use of correct sentence formation, punctuation, capitalization, grammar usage, and spelling
NS	> Insufficient (includes copied text) > In a language other than English > Off-topic > Off-purpose

Holistic Scoring:

> **Variety:** A range of errors includes sentence formation, punctuation, capitalization, grammar usage, and spelling.

> **Severity:** Basic errors are more heavily weighted than higher-level errors.

> **Density:** The proportion of errors to the amount of writing done well. This includes the ratio of errors to the length of the piece.

	4-Point Narrative Performance Task Writing Rubric (Grades 3–8)
Score	Purpose/Organization
4	**The organization of the narrative, real or imagined, is fully sustained and the focus is clear and maintained throughout:** > an effective plot helps to create a sense of unity and completeness > effectively establishes a setting, narrator/characters, and/or point of view* > consistent use of a variety of transitional strategies to clarify the relationships between and among ideas; strong connection between and among ideas > natural, logical sequence of events from beginning to end > effective opening and closure for audience and purpose
3	**The organization of the narrative, real or imagined, is adequately sustained, and the focus is adequate and generally maintained:** > an evident plot helps to create a sense of unity and completeness, though there may be minor flaws and some ideas may be loosely connected > adequately establishes a setting, narrator/characters, and/or point of view* > adequate use of a variety of transitional strategies to clarify the relationships between and among ideas > adequate sequence of events from beginning to end > adequate opening and closure for audience and purpose
2	**The organization of the narrative, real or imagined, is somewhat sustained and may have an uneven focus:** > there may be an inconsistent plot, and/or flaws may be evident > unevenly or minimally establishes a setting, narrator/characters, and/or point of view* > uneven use of appropriate transitional strategies and/or little variety > weak or uneven sequence of events > opening and closure, if present, are weak

1	The organization of the narrative, real or imagined, may be maintained but may provide little or no focus:
	> there is little or no discernible plot or there may just be a series of events
	> may be brief or there is little to no attempt to establish a setting, narrator/characters, and/or point of view*
	> few or no appropriate transitional strategies may be evident and may cause confusion
	> little or no organization of an event sequence; frequent extraneous ideas and/or a major drift may be evident
	> opening and/or closure may be missing or unsatisfactory
NS	> Insufficient (includes copied text)
	> In a language other than English
	> Off-topic
	> Off-purpose

*Point of view begins at grade 7.

Score	Development/Elaboration
4	The narrative, real or imagined, provides thorough, effective elaboration using relevant details, dialogue, and/or description:
	> experiences, characters, setting, and/or events are clearly developed
	> connections to source materials may enhance the narrative
	> effective use of a variety of narrative techniques that advance the story or illustrate the experience
	> effective use of sensory, concrete, and figurative language that clearly advances the purpose
	> effective, appropriate style enhances the narration
3	The narrative, real or imagined, provides adequate elaboration using details, dialogue, and/or description:
	> experiences, characters, setting, and/or events are adequately developed
	> connections to source materials may contribute to the narrative
	> adequate use of a variety of narrative techniques that generally advance the story or illustrate the experience
	> adequate use of sensory, concrete, and figurative language that generally advances the purpose
	> generally appropriate style is evident

2	The narrative, real or imagined, provides uneven, cursory elaboration using partial and uneven details, dialogue, and/or description:
	> experiences, characters, setting, and/or events are unevenly developed
	> connections to source materials may be ineffective, awkward, or vague but do not interfere with the narrative
	> narrative techniques are uneven and inconsistent
	> partial or weak use of sensory, concrete, and figurative language that may not advance the purpose
	> inconsistent or weak attempt to create appropriate style
1	The narrative, real or imagined, provides minimal elaboration using few or no details, dialogue, and/or description:
	> experiences, characters, setting, and/or events may be vague, lack clarity, or confusing
	> connections to source materials, if evident, may detract from the narrative
	> use of narrative techniques may be minimal, absent, incorrect, or irrelevant
	> may have little or no use of sensory, concrete, or figurative language; language does not advance and may interfere with the purpose
	> little or no evidence of appropriate style
NS	> Insufficient (includes copied text)
	> In a language other than English
	> Off-topic
	> Off-purpose

	2-Point Narrative Performance Task Writing Rubric (Grades 3–8)
Score	Conventions
2	**The response demonstrates an adequate command of conventions:** > adequate use of correct sentence formation, punctuation, capitalization, grammar usage, and spelling
1	**The response demonstrates a partial command of conventions:** > limited use of correct sentence formation, punctuation, capitalization, grammar usage, and spelling
0	**The response demonstrates little or no command of conventions:** > infrequent use of correct sentence formation, punctuation, capitalization, grammar usage, and spelling
NS	> Insufficient (includes copied text) > In a language other than English > Off-topic > Off-purpose

Holistic Scoring:
> **Variety:** A range of errors includes sentence formation, punctuation, capitalization, grammar usage, and spelling.
> **Severity:** Basic errors are more heavily weighted than higher-level errors.
> **Density:** The proportion of errors to the amount of writing done well. This includes the ratio of errors to the length of the piece.

Grade 8 English Language Arts Common Core Standards

College and Career Readiness Anchor Standards for Reading
Key Ideas and Details
CCSS.ELA-LITERACY.CCRA.R.1 Read closely to determine what the text says explicitly and to make logical inferences from it; cite specific textual evidence when writing or speaking to support conclusions drawn from the text.
CCSS.ELA-LITERACY.CCRA.R.2 Determine central ideas or themes of a text and analyze their development; summarize the key supporting details and ideas.
CCSS.ELA-LITERACY.CCRA.R.3 Analyze how and why individuals, events, or ideas develop and interact over the course of a text.
Craft and Structure
CCSS.ELA-LITERACY.CCRA.R.4 Interpret words and phrases as they are used in a text, including determining technical, connotative, and figurative meanings, and analyze how specific word choices shape meaning or tone.
CCSS.ELA-LITERACY.CCRA.R.5 Analyze the structure of texts, including how specific sentences, paragraphs, and larger portions of the text (e.g., a section, chapter, scene, or stanza) relate to each other and the whole.
CCSS.ELA-LITERACY.CCRA.R.6 Assess how point of view or purpose shapes the content and style of a text.

Integration of Knowledge and Ideas

CCSS.ELA-LITERACY.CCRA.R.7 Integrate and evaluate content presented in diverse media and formats, including visually and quantitatively, as well as in words.

CCSS.ELA-LITERACY.CCRA.R.8 Delineate and evaluate the argument and specific claims in a text, including the validity of the reasoning as well as the relevance and sufficiency of the evidence.

CCSS.ELA-LITERACY.CCRA.R.9 Analyze how two or more texts address similar themes or topics in order to build knowledge or to compare the approaches the authors take.

Range of Reading and Level of Text Complexity

CCSS.ELA-LITERACY.CCRA.R.10 Read and comprehend complex literary and informational texts independently and proficiently.

College and Career Readiness Anchor Standards for Writing

Text Types and Purposes

CCSS.ELA-LITERACY.CCRA.W.1 Write arguments to support claims in an analysis of substantive topics or texts using valid reasoning and relevant and sufficient evidence.

CCSS.ELA-LITERACY.CCRA.W.2 Write informative/explanatory texts to examine and convey complex ideas and information clearly and accurately through the effective selection, organization, and analysis of content.

CCSS.ELA-LITERACY.CCRA.W.3 Write narratives to develop real or imagined experiences or events using effective technique, well-chosen details, and well-structured event sequences.

Production and Distribution of Writing

CCSS.ELA-LITERACY.CCRA.W.4 Produce clear and coherent writing in which the development, organization, and style are appropriate to task, purpose, and audience.

CCSS.ELA-LITERACY.CCRA.W.5 Develop and strengthen writing as needed by planning, revising, editing, rewriting, or trying a new approach.

CCSS.ELA-LITERACY.CCRA.W.6 Use technology, including the Internet, to produce and publish writing and to interact and collaborate with others.

Research to Build and Present Knowledge

CCSS.ELA-LITERACY.CCRA.W.7 Conduct short as well as more sustained research projects based on focused questions, demonstrating understanding of the subject under investigation.

CCSS.ELA-LITERACY.CCRA.W.8 Gather relevant information from multiple print and digital sources, assess the credibility and accuracy of each source, and integrate the information while avoiding plagiarism.

CCSS.ELA-LITERACY.CCRA.W.9 Draw evidence from literary or informational texts to support analysis, reflection, and research.

Range of Writing

CCSS.ELA-LITERACY.CCRA.W.10 Write routinely over extended time frames (time for research, reflection, and revision) and shorter time frames (a single sitting or a day or two) for a range of tasks, purposes, and audiences.

College and Career Readiness Anchor Standards for Speaking and Listening

Comprehension and Collaboration

CCSS.ELA-LITERACY.CCRA.SL.1 Prepare for and participate effectively in a range of conversations and collaborations with diverse partners, building on others' ideas and expressing their own clearly and persuasively.

CCSS.ELA-LITERACY.CCRA.SL.2 Integrate and evaluate information presented in diverse media and formats, including visually, quantitatively, and orally.

CCSS.ELA-LITERACY.CCRA.SL.3 Evaluate a speaker's point of view, reasoning, and use of evidence and rhetoric.

Presentation of Knowledge and Ideas

CCSS.ELA-LITERACY.CCRA.SL.4 Present information, findings, and supporting evidence such that listeners can follow the line of reasoning and the organization, development, and style are appropriate to task, purpose, and audience.

CCSS.ELA-LITERACY.CCRA.SL.5 Make strategic use of digital media and visual displays of data to express information and enhance understanding of presentations.

CCSS.ELA-LITERACY.CCRA.SL.6 Adapt speech to a variety of contexts and communicative tasks, demonstrating command of formal English when indicated or appropriate.

College and Career Readiness Anchor Standards for Language

Conventions of Standard English

CCSS.ELA-LITERACY.CCRA.L.1 Demonstrate command of the conventions of standard English grammar and usage when writing or speaking.

CCSS.ELA-LITERACY.CCRA.L.2 Demonstrate command of the conventions of standard English capitalization, punctuation, and spelling when writing.

Knowledge of Language

CCSS.ELA-LITERACY.CCRA.L.3 Apply knowledge of language to understand how language functions in different contexts, to make effective choices for meaning or style, and to comprehend more fully when reading or listening.

Vocabulary Acquisition and Use

CCSS.ELA-LITERACY.CCRA.L.4 Determine or clarify the meaning of unknown and multiple-meaning words and phrases by using context clues, analyzing meaningful word parts, and consulting general and specialized reference materials, as appropriate.

CCSS.ELA-LITERACY.CCRA.L.5 Demonstrate understanding of figurative language, word relationships, and nuances in word meanings.

CCSS.ELA-LITERACY.CCRA.L.6 Acquire and use accurately a range of general academic and domain-specific words and phrases sufficient for reading, writing, speaking, and listening at the college and career readiness level; demonstrate independence in gathering vocabulary knowledge when encountering an unknown term important to comprehension or expression.

Reading: Literature

Key Ideas and Details

CCSS.ELA-LITERACY.RL.8.1 Cite the textual evidence that most strongly supports an analysis of what the text says explicitly as well as inferences drawn from the text.

CCSS.ELA-LITERACY.RL.8.2 Determine a theme or central idea of a text and analyze its development over the course of the text, including its relationship to the characters, setting, and plot; provide an objective summary of the text.

CCSS.ELA-LITERACY.RL.8.3 Analyze how particular lines of dialogue or incidents in a story or drama propel the action, reveal aspects of a character, or provoke a decision.

Craft and Structure

CCSS.ELA-LITERACY.RL.8.4 Determine the meaning of words and phrases as they are used in a text, including figurative and connotative meanings; analyze the impact of specific word choices on meaning and tone, including analogies or allusions to other texts.

CCSS.ELA-LITERACY.RL.8.5 Compare and contrast the structure of two or more texts and analyze how the differing structure of each text contributes to its meaning and style.

CCSS.ELA-LITERACY.RL.8.6 Analyze how differences in the points of view of the characters and the audience or reader (e.g., created through the use of dramatic irony) create such effects as suspense or humor.

Integration of Knowledge and Ideas

CCSS.ELA-LITERACY.RL.8.7 Analyze the extent to which a filmed or live production of a story or drama stays faithful to or departs from the text or script, evaluating the choices made by the director or actors.

CCSS.ELA-LITERACY.RL.8.8 (RL.8.8 not applicable to literature)

CCSS.ELA-LITERACY.RL.8.9 Analyze how a modern work of fiction draws on themes, patterns of events, or character types from myths, traditional stories, or religious works such as the Bible, including describing how the material is rendered new.

Range of Reading and Level of Text Complexity

CCSS.ELA-LITERACY.RL.8.10 By the end of the year, read and comprehend literature, including stories, dramas, and poems, at the high end of grades 6–8 text complexity band independently and proficiently.

Reading: Informational Text

Key Ideas and Details

CCSS.ELA-LITERACY.RI.8.1 Cite the textual evidence that most strongly supports an analysis of what the text says explicitly as well as inferences drawn from the text.

CCSS.ELA-LITERACY.RI.8.2 Determine a central idea of a text and analyze its development over the course of the text, including its relationship to supporting ideas; provide an objective summary of the text.

CCSS.ELA-LITERACY.RI.8.3 Analyze how a text makes connections among and distinctions between individuals, ideas, or events (e.g., through comparisons, analogies, or categories).

Craft and Structure

CCSS.ELA-LITERACY.RI.8.4 Determine the meaning of words and phrases as they are used in a text, including figurative, connotative, and technical meanings; analyze the impact of specific word choices on meaning and tone, including analogies or allusions to other texts.

CCSS.ELA-LITERACY.RI.8.5 Analyze in detail the structure of a specific paragraph in a text, including the role of particular sentences in developing and refining a key concept.

CCSS.ELA-LITERACY.RI.8.6 Determine an author's point of view or purpose in a text and analyze how the author acknowledges and responds to conflicting evidence or viewpoints.

Integration of Knowledge and Ideas

CCSS.ELA-LITERACY.RI.8.7 Evaluate the advantages and disadvantages of using different mediums (e.g., print or digital text, video, multimedia) to present a particular topic or idea.

CCSS.ELA-LITERACY.RI.8.8 Delineate and evaluate the argument and specific claims in a text, assessing whether the reasoning is sound and the evidence is relevant and sufficient; recognize when irrelevant evidence is introduced.

CCSS.ELA-LITERACY.RI.8.9 Analyze a case in which two or more texts provide conflicting information on the same topic and identify where the texts disagree on matters of fact or interpretation.

Range of Reading and Level of Text Complexity

CCSS.ELA-LITERACY.RI.8.10 By the end of the year, read and comprehend literary nonfiction at the high end of the grades 6–8 text complexity band independently and proficiently.

Writing

Text Types and Purposes

CCSS.ELA-LITERACY.W.8.1 Write arguments to support claims with clear reasons and relevant evidence.

CCSS.ELA-LITERACY.W.8.1.A Introduce claim(s), acknowledge and distinguish the claim(s) from alternate or opposing claims, and organize the reasons and evidence logically.

CCSS.ELA-LITERACY.W.8.1.B Support claim(s) with logical reasoning and relevant evidence, using accurate, credible sources and demonstrating an understanding of the topic or text.

CCSS.ELA-LITERACY.W.8.1.C Use words, phrases, and clauses to create cohesion and clarify the relationships among claim(s), counterclaims, reasons, and evidence.

CCSS.ELA-LITERACY.W.8.1.D Establish and maintain a formal style.

CCSS.ELA-LITERACY.W.8.1.E Provide a concluding statement or section that follows from and supports the argument presented.

CCSS.ELA-LITERACY.W.8.2 Write informative/explanatory texts to examine a topic and convey ideas, concepts, and information through the selection, organization, and analysis of relevant content.

CCSS.ELA-LITERACY.W.8.2.A Introduce a topic clearly, previewing what is to follow; organize ideas, concepts, and information into broader categories; include formatting (e.g., headings), graphics (e.g., charts, tables), and multimedia when useful to aiding comprehension.

CCSS.ELA-LITERACY.W.8.2.B Develop the topic with relevant, well-chosen facts, definitions, concrete details, quotations, or other information and examples.

CCSS.ELA-LITERACY.W.8.2.C Use appropriate and varied transitions to create cohesion and clarify the relationships among ideas and concepts.

CCSS.ELA-LITERACY.W.8.2.D Use precise language and domain-specific vocabulary to inform about or explain the topic.

CCSS.ELA-LITERACY.W.8.2.E Establish and maintain a formal style.

CCSS.ELA-LITERACY.W.8.2.F Provide a concluding statement or section that follows from and supports the information or explanation presented.

CCSS.ELA-LITERACY.W.8.3 Write narratives to develop real or imagined experiences or events using effective technique, relevant descriptive details, and well-structured event sequences.

CCSS.ELA-LITERACY.W.8.3.A Engage and orient the reader by establishing a context and point of view and introducing a narrator and/or characters; organize an event sequence that unfolds naturally and logically.

CCSS.ELA-LITERACY.W.8.3.B Use narrative techniques, such as dialogue, pacing, description, and reflection, to develop experiences, events, and/or characters.

CCSS.ELA-LITERACY.W.8.3.C Use a variety of transition words, phrases, and clauses to convey sequence, signal shifts from one time frame or setting to another, and show the relationships among experiences and events.

CCSS.ELA-LITERACY.W.8.3.D Use precise words and phrases, relevant descriptive details, and sensory language to capture the action and convey experiences and events.

CCSS.ELA-LITERACY.W.8.3.E Provide a conclusion that follows from and reflects on the narrated experiences or events.

Production and Distribution of Writing

CCSS.ELA-LITERACY.W.8.4 Produce clear and coherent writing in which the development, organization, and style are appropriate to task, purpose, and audience. (Grade-specific expectations for writing types are defined in standards 1–3 above.)

CCSS.ELA-LITERACY.W.8.5 With some guidance and support from peers and adults, develop and strengthen writing as needed by planning, revising, editing, rewriting, or trying a new approach, focusing on how well purpose and audience have been addressed. (Editing for conventions should demonstrate command of Language standards 1–3 up to and including grade 8.)

CCSS.ELA-LITERACY.W.8.6 Use technology, including the Internet, to produce and publish writing and present the relationships between information and ideas efficiently as well as to interact and collaborate with others.

Research to Build and Present Knowledge

CCSS.ELA-LITERACY.W.8.7 Conduct short research projects to answer a question (including a self-generated question), drawing on several sources and generating additional related, focused questions that allow for multiple avenues of exploration.

CCSS.ELA-LITERACY.W.8.8 Gather relevant information from multiple print and digital sources, using search terms effectively; assess the credibility and accuracy of each source; and quote or paraphrase the data and conclusions of others while avoiding plagiarism and following a standard format for citation.

CCSS.ELA-LITERACY.W.8.9 Draw evidence from literary or informational texts to support analysis, reflection, and research.

> **CCSS.ELA-LITERACY.W.8.9.A** Apply *grade 8 Reading standards* to literature (e.g., "Analyze how a modern work of fiction draws on themes, patterns of events, or character types from myths, traditional stories, or religious works such as the Bible, including describing how the material is rendered new").

> **CCSS.ELA-LITERACY.W.8.9.B** Apply *grade 8 Reading standards* to literary nonfiction (e.g., "Delineate and evaluate the argument and specific claims in a text, assessing whether the reasoning is sound and the evidence is relevant and sufficient; recognize when irrelevant evidence is introduced").

Range of Writing

CCSS.ELA-LITERACY.W.8.10 Write routinely over extended time frames (time for research, reflection, and revision) and shorter time frames (a single sitting or a day or two) for a range of discipline-specific tasks, purposes, and audiences.

Speaking & Listening

Comprehension and Collaboration

CCSS.ELA-LITERACY.SL.8.1 Engage effectively in a range of collaborative discussions (one-on-one, in groups, and teacher-led) with diverse partners on grade 8 topics, texts, and issues, building on others' ideas and expressing their own clearly.

CCSS.ELA-LITERACY.SL.8.1.A Come to discussions prepared, having read or researched material under study; explicitly draw on that preparation by referring to evidence on the topic, text, or issue to probe and reflect on ideas under discussion.

CCSS.ELA-LITERACY.SL.8.1.B Follow rules for collegial discussions and decision-making, track progress toward specific goals and deadlines, and define individual roles as needed.

CCSS.ELA-LITERACY.SL.8.1.C Pose questions that connect the ideas of several speakers and respond to others' questions and comments with relevant evidence, observations, and ideas.

CCSS.ELA-LITERACY.SL.8.1.D Acknowledge new information expressed by others, and, when warranted, qualify or justify their own views in light of the evidence presented.

CCSS.ELA-LITERACY.SL.8.2 Analyze the purpose of information presented in diverse media and formats (e.g., visually, quantitatively, orally) and evaluate the motives (e.g., social, commercial, political) behind its presentation.

CCSS.ELA-LITERACY.SL.8.3 Delineate a speaker's argument and specific claims, evaluating the soundness of the reasoning and relevance and sufficiency of the evidence and identifying when irrelevant evidence is introduced.

Presentation of Knowledge and Ideas

CCSS.ELA-LITERACY.SL.8.4 Present claims and findings, emphasizing salient points in a focused, coherent manner with relevant evidence, sound valid reasoning, and well-chosen details; use appropriate eye contact, adequate volume, and clear pronunciation.

CCSS.ELA-LITERACY.SL.8.5 Integrate multimedia and visual displays into presentations to clarify information, strengthen claims and evidence, and add interest.

CCSS.ELA-LITERACY.SL.8.6 Adapt speech to a variety of contexts and tasks, demonstrating command of formal English when indicated or appropriate. (See grade 8 Language standards 1 and 3 for specific expectations.)

Language

Conventions of Standard English

CCSS.ELA-LITERACY.L.8.1 Demonstrate command of the conventions of standard English grammar and usage when writing or speaking.

> **CCSS.ELA-LITERACY.L.8.1.A** Explain the function of verbals (gerunds, participles, infinitives) in general and their function in particular sentences.

> **CCSS.ELA-LITERACY.L.8.1.B** Form and use verbs in the active and passive voice.

> **CCSS.ELA-LITERACY.L.8.1.C** Form and use verbs in the indicative, imperative, interrogative, conditional, and subjunctive mood.

> **CCSS.ELA-LITERACY.L.8.1.D** Recognize and correct inappropriate shifts in verb voice and mood.

CCSS.ELA-LITERACY.L.8.2 Demonstrate command of the conventions of standard English capitalization, punctuation, and spelling when writing.

> **CCSS.ELA-LITERACY.L.8.2.A** Use punctuation (comma, ellipsis, dash) to indicate a pause or break.

> **CCSS.ELA-LITERACY.L.8.2.B** Use an ellipsis to indicate an omission.

> **CCSS.ELA-LITERACY.L.8.2.C** Spell correctly.

Knowledge of Language

CCSS.ELA-LITERACY.L.8.3 Use knowledge of language and its conventions when writing, speaking, reading, or listening.

> **CCSS.ELA-LITERACY.L.8.3.A** Use verbs in the active and passive voice and in the conditional and subjunctive mood to achieve particular effects (e.g., emphasizing the actor or the action; expressing uncertainty or describing a state contrary to fact).

Vocabulary Acquisition and Use

CCSS.ELA-LITERACY.L.8.4 Determine or clarify the meaning of unknown and multiple-meaning words or phrases based on *grade 8 reading and content*, choosing flexibly from a range of strategies.

> **CCSS.ELA-LITERACY.L.8.4.A** Use context (e.g., the overall meaning of a sentence or paragraph; a word's position or function in a sentence) as a clue to the meaning of a word or phrase.

CCSS.ELA-LITERACY.L.8.4.B Use common, grade-appropriate Greek or Latin affixes and roots as clues to the meaning of a word (e.g., *precede, recede, secede*).

CCSS.ELA-LITERACY.L.8.4.C Consult general and specialized reference materials (e.g., dictionaries, glossaries, thesauruses), both print and digital, to find the pronunciation of a word or determine or clarify its precise meaning or its part of speech.

CCSS.ELA-LITERACY.L.8.4.D Verify the preliminary determination of the meaning of a word or phrase (e.g., by checking the inferred meaning in context or in a dictionary).

CCSS.ELA-LITERACY.L.8.5 Demonstrate understanding of figurative language, word relationships, and nuances in word meanings.

CCSS.ELA-LITERACY.L.8.5.A Interpret figures of speech (e.g., verbal irony, puns) in context.

CCSS.ELA-LITERACY.L.8.5.B Use the relationship between particular words to better understand each of the words.

CCSS.ELA-LITERACY.L.8.5.C Distinguish among the connotations (associations) of words with similar denotations (definitions) (e.g., *bullheaded, willful, firm, persistent, resolute*).

CCSS.ELA-LITERACY.L.8.6 Acquire and use accurately grade-appropriate general academic and domain-specific words and phrases; gather vocabulary knowledge when considering a word or phrase important to comprehension or expression.

Glossary

Achievement levels—Four levels in each of the four claim areas that are part of the final scoring. Level 4 is considered exceeding the standards. Level 3 is considered meeting the standards. Level 2 is considered nearly meeting the standards. Level 1 Is consIdered not meeting the standards.

Argumentative response task—One of three constructed-response tasks that requires you to include a claim, solid reasoning, and relevant support for the claim. This task also asks you to consider counterarguments from opposing points of view. These tasks may sometimes be referred to as "persuasive writing" by your teachers.

Claim—The main idea in your writing. Teachers may also call the claim the "thesis statement."

Common Core Standards—These are the learning standards on which you will be tested by the SBAC. They include knowledge and skills that you are to master during the school year. A complete list of the Grade 8 English Language Arts Common Core Standards is available in Appendix B.

Computer Adaptive Test (CAT)—A computer test that adjusts the questions depending on whether you answer questions correctly or incorrectly. If you answer a CAT item correctly, the next item will be adjusted to the next level of difficulty, or the level of difficulty could stay the same as for the previous question. If you answer a CAT item incorrectly, the level of difficulty could either stay the same as for the previous question or drop. The test will continue to adapt to the right level for you. Note that the CAT will include selected-response tasks, technology-enhanced tasks, and constructed-response tasks.

Constructed-response task—These tasks require you to construct a brief written response after you examine a text or any other non-text stimulus (such as a picture, a graph, a chart, a video clip, etc.). The stimulus could be from any genre, and it could be fiction or nonfiction.

ELA—English Language Arts, which includes reading, writing, speaking, listening, analyzing, and researching.

Embedded universal tools—These tools are located within the computer testing program and include such tools as the highlighter, text zooming, and other computer features.

Explanatory response—One of three constructed-response tasks that requires you to include a claim and relevant support for the claim as you explain an idea.

Narrative response—One of three constructed-response tasks that requires you to write a real or imagined story.

Non-embedded universal tools—These tools are located outside of the computer testing program and include such tools as a physical dictionary, scratch paper, and a physical thesaurus.

Non-traditional response—See technology-enhanced task.

Orientation—One of the testing strategies in which you read the overview and the tasks carefully first (skipping the stimulus text for now) to gain a better idea of what the tasks will require and include.

Performance Task—This section of the SBAC Grade 8 ELA exam includes two sessions: an information-gathering session (see the Performance Task lesson) and a session in which you read source material and write a response. The writing sample could include either an explanatory or argumentative essay or a real or imagined narrative.

Performance Task lesson—The classroom lesson (which usually lasts approximately 30 minutes) is presented by a teacher in preparation for the second session of the Performance Task, which involves reading source material and writing a response.

SBAC—Smarter Balanced Assessment Consortium. The SBAC Grade 8 ELA exam measures the full range of your abilities in the Common Core Standards practiced during eighth grade.

SBAC claims—The four overall goals and the purpose of the SBAC test.

Scaled score—The overall numerical score for the SBAC test, which falls on a continuous scale (from approximately 2000 to 3000) that increases across grade levels.

Scoring rubric—The descriptions for each score point for an item/task that scores more than one point for a correct response.

Selected-response task—These are essentially multiple-choice questions.

Stem—The statement of the question or prompt to which you will need to respond.

Stimulus—The source about which the item/task is written. The stimulus text can come from any genre. You may be asked to read a poem, a narrative, or an informative text. You might also be asked to view or listen to some other form of media such as a video clip, an audio clip, a graph, a chart, or an image.

Strikethrough—An embedded universal tool with which you can virtually cross out answer options to help narrow down the options for the correct answer. If an answer choice is an image, a strikethrough line will not appear, but the image will be grayed out.

Technology-enhanced task—These types of tasks can only be performed on a computer since they require the test taker to use computer technology (such as clicking on a part of a passage) to complete the task.

Testing administrator—The adult who will run the test. The testing administrator is usually your teacher.

Index